CHILDREN

A parent's guide on how to keep children
safe in a digital world.

DEDICATION

This book is dedicated to everyone trying to navigate the Cybersecurity Landscape, whether you are a cybersecurity professional or a cybersecurity novice. We at Cybersnap hope "DIGITAL. A Parents Guide to the Digital Landscape and How to Keep Children Safe in a Digital World" gives you the tools to keep you and your family safe against cyber threats.

This book addresses bullying and human trafficking, prevalent issues for children and anyone online today.

INTRODUCTION

In an increasingly interconnected world, where digital devices and the online realm play an integral role in our lives, ensuring the safety and security of our children has taken on a whole new dimension. This book is meant to be a comprehensive guide crafted to assist parents in confidently navigating the complex landscape of cybersecurity for their children.

Rapid technological advancements have ushered in a new era of opportunities and challenges. From online education and entertainment to social networking and communication, our children are more digitally connected than ever before. However, this connectivity has potential risks that parents must be equipped to address. This book is a beacon of knowledge, helping parents understand, manage, and mitigate the cybersecurity concerns surrounding their children's digital experiences.

Within these pages, we delve into essential topics that bridge the gap between parents and the world of cybersecurity. We explore the importance of open communication with your children about online safety, offering practical advice on fostering healthy digital habits and establishing trust-based relationships in the virtual realm.

From understanding the potential dangers of social media and online gaming to recognizing the signs of cyberbullying and internet addiction, this book provides insights that empower parents to identify and address threats effectively. You will discover actionable strategies for safeguarding personal information, managing privacy settings, and educating your children about responsible online behaviour.

Whether you're a tech-savvy parent seeking to enhance your child's online safety or a guardian looking to bridge the digital divide, this book offers a roadmap to nurture responsible, secure, and enjoyable digital experiences for your children.

As we embark on this journey together, we promise to illuminate the path to creating a digital environment where our children can flourish, explore, and connect while staying safe from the ever-evolving challenges of the online realm.

PUBLISHERS NOTE

Cybersnap is an award-winning Cybersecurity organization co-founded by Gregory Dharma LePard, its Chief Evangelist and Cybersecurity expert and Imogen Fannon, Chief Engagement Officer and philanthropy advocate. At Cybersnap, we believe cybersecurity education should be accessible and available to all and in a format understood by all to educate and protect you, the reader, as you explore the ever-evolving cyber landscape.

A portion of the proceeds from this book will be donated to **Girls Inc. Durham**.

For more information, visit: **https://girlsinc.org/**

This book provides information for general and educational purposes only and is not a substitute for professional advice. Accordingly, we encourage you to consult with the appropriate professionals or do your research before taking any actions based on such information.

First Edition

Table Contents

CHAPTER 1: UNDERSTANDING THE DIGITAL LANDSCAPE

Section 1: The Benefits of the Digital World

Connectivity and Communication

The internet has revolutionized the way children connect with others, allowing them to forge relationships and foster communication and collaboration on a global scale. Here are some key points to consider:

1. *Global Reach:* The internet breaks down geographical barriers, enabling children to connect with friends, family, and peers from around the world. Through social media platforms, instant messaging apps, and video conferencing tools, children can communicate and interact with individuals they wouldn't have had the opportunity to meet otherwise.

2. *Enhanced Communication:* The internet provides various avenues for communication, including email, messaging apps, video calls, and social media. Children can engage in real-time conversations, share experiences, and maintain ongoing connections with friends and family, regardless of physical location.

3. *Cultural Exchange:* The internet allows children to engage in cultural exchange by connecting with individuals from diverse backgrounds and cultures. They can learn about different traditions, languages, and customs, fostering a global perspective and promoting cultural understanding and empathy.

4. *Collaborative Learning:* The internet facilitates collaboration among children for educational purposes. Online platforms allow students to collaborate on projects, exchange ideas, and work together on assignments. This promotes teamwork, communication skills, and cross-cultural understanding, preparing children for their interconnected world.

5. *Support Networks:* The internet provides a platform for children to connect with others who share similar interests, hobbies, or challenges. Online communities, forums, and support groups allow children to find like-minded individuals and seek advice, support, and encouragement. These connections can be especially valuable for children who may feel isolated offline.

6. *Creative Expression and Showcasing Talents:* Children can share their creative endeavours with a global audience through the Internet. They can showcase their artwork, writing, music, or other talents on social media, blogs, or dedicated platforms. This boosts their self-confidence and provides feedback, collaboration, and recognition opportunities.

7. *Language Learning:* The Internet offers various language-learning resources, including language exchange platforms, interactive courses, and virtual language communities. Children can connect with native speakers, practice their language skills, and immerse themselves in different languages and cultures, enhancing their linguistic abilities.

It's important for parents to guide their children in navigating online connections responsibly. Establishing clear guidelines and boundaries, discussing online safety measures, and fostering open communication about online interactions can ensure that children benefit from the positive aspects of connecting with others while staying safe in the digital world.

Access to Information and Learning

The internet offers abundant resources for educational purposes, research, and expanding knowledge across a wide range of subjects. Here are some key highlights:

1. *Information and Reference Materials*: Online platforms provide access to vast amounts of information, making it easier for children to conduct research and explore various topics. Websites, online encyclopedias, and digital libraries offer articles, e-books, scholarly papers, and multimedia content catering to different learning styles.

2. *Educational Websites and Learning Platforms:* Numerous websites and platforms are dedicated to educational content. These platforms offer interactive lessons, quizzes, tutorials, and exercises that cover subjects ranging from math and science to language learning and history. They often employ engaging techniques such as gamification and multimedia elements to enhance the learning experience.

3. *Open Educational Resources:* Open educational resources (OER) are freely accessible materials available online for educational purposes. These resources include textbooks, lecture notes, videos, and simulations that students, teachers, and parents can use to supplement traditional learning materials. OER platforms provide rich educational content across various subjects and grade levels.

4. *Online Courses and Webinars:* The internet has made learning more accessible through online courses and webinars. Reputable platforms offer courses on various topics, allowing children to explore their interests or delve

11

deeper into subjects not covered in their regular curriculum. These courses often provide interactive elements, assessments, and opportunities for collaboration with other learners.

5. *Virtual Museums and Exhibitions:* Many museums and cultural institutions have embraced the digital realm, offering virtual tours and exhibitions. Children can explore famous museums, historical sites, and art collections from around the world without leaving their homes. These virtual experiences provide a unique opportunity to learn about history, art, and culture in an engaging and immersive manner.

6. *STEM Resources and Coding Platforms:* The internet provides resources and tools specifically designed for STEM (Science, Technology, Engineering, and Mathematics) education. Online platforms offer coding tutorials, virtual labs, simulations, and experiments that help children develop critical thinking, problem-solving, and computational thinking skills.

7. *Multimedia and Interactive Learning:* The internet offers many multimedia resources, including educational videos, podcasts, infographics, and interactive simulations. These resources cater to different learning styles and can make complex concepts more accessible and engaging for children.

8. *Online Communities and Forums:* Online communities and forums dedicated to specific subjects or academic interests allow children to connect with fellow learners, experts, and enthusiasts. These platforms provide opportunities for discussions, knowledge sharing, and

collaborative learning, fostering a sense of community and expanding children's perspectives.

Parents can support their children in utilizing these online educational resources by finding reliable sources, teaching them how to evaluate information critically, and helping them navigate the digital landscape responsibly. Children can enhance their educational journey and expand their knowledge in diverse subjects by harnessing vast online resources.

Creativity and Expression

Digital platforms offer children numerous opportunities to express themselves creatively in various art forms, including art, writing, music, and more. Here's an exploration of how these platforms empower children's creative expression:

1. *Visual Art: Digital Drawing and Painting:* Drawing and painting applications and software provide children with a digital canvas to create artwork using virtual brushes, colours, and tools. They can experiment with different styles, techniques, and effects, allowing endless possibilities and creative exploration.

2. *Digital Photography:* Children can use digital cameras or smartphones to capture images and then edit and enhance them using photo editing software. They can experiment with composition, lighting, and various artistic filters to convey their unique perspective and tell visual stories.

3. *Writing and Literature:* Blogging and Online Journals: Digital platforms allow children to share their thoughts, stories, and ideas through personal blogs or online journals. They can publish their writing, receive feedback from readers, and connect with other young writers, fostering a sense of community and inspiring further creativity.

4. *Creative Writing Platforms:* Online platforms dedicated to creative writing provide children with prompts, challenges, and opportunities to participate in writing competitions. They can explore different genres, develop storytelling skills, and receive feedback from peers or mentors.

5. *Music and Sound: Music Composition Software:* Digital music composition software allows children to create and compose music using virtual instruments, synthesizers, and mixing tools. They can experiment with melodies, rhythms, and sound effects, expressing themselves through original compositions.

6. *Podcasting and Audio Storytelling:* Children can create and share podcasts or audio stories using digital platforms. They can narrate stories, record interviews, or explore topics of interest, using sound effects and music to enhance the storytelling experience.

7. *Digital Design and Multimedia:* Graphic Design and Illustration: Digital design tools enable children to create digital graphics, illustrations, and visual elements. They can design posters, logos, digital art, or even develop animations, expressing their creativity visually.

8. *Video Creation and Editing:* Children can create videos by filming, editing, and adding visual effects using video editing software. They can produce short films, animations, or video essays to communicate their ideas and stories.

9. *Online Communities and Collaborations: Social Media and Online Platforms:* Children can share their creative works on social media platforms dedicated to art, writing,

music, or other creative disciplines. They can connect with like-minded individuals, receive feedback, and find inspiration from others' creations.

10. *Collaborative Projects and Remixing:* Digital platforms enable children to collaborate on creative projects with others, even if they are geographically distant. They can remix artwork, music, or writing with others, combining different perspectives and styles to create something new and unique.

By leveraging digital platforms, children can showcase their creativity, gain recognition, and connect with a wider audience. It encourages them to explore their artistic passions, develop their skills, and build confidence in expressing themselves through various creative outlets.

Opportunities for children to express themselves through art, writing, music, and other creative outlets

The internet allows children to express themselves creatively through art, writing, music, and other outlets. Here are some specific ways they can leverage the Internet for creative expression:

1. *Art and Design: Online Art Communities:* Children can join online art communities and platforms dedicated to showcasing artwork. They can share their creations, receive feedback, and connect with other young artists, fostering inspiration and collaboration.

2. *Digital Art Platforms:* Children can explore digital art tools and software that allow them to create digital illustrations, animations, or graphic designs. They can experiment with different techniques and styles, sharing their artwork online with a global audience.

3. ***Writing and Literature:*** Blogging and Online Writing Platforms: Children can start blogs or participate in online writing platforms to publish their stories, poems, or articles. They can receive feedback from readers and engage in discussions with fellow young writers.

4. ***Writing Contests and Challenges:*** Online platforms host writing contests and challenges for children and teenagers. These platforms provide themes or prompts, encouraging young writers to explore different genres and improve their writing skills.

5. ***Music and Sound: Music Creation Software:*** Children can use music creation software and digital audio workstations (DAWs) to compose and produce music. They can experiment with different instruments, beats, and sounds to create original compositions.

6. ***Online Music Communities:*** Children can join online communities dedicated to music creation and sharing. They can showcase their musical talents, collaborate with other musicians, and receive feedback from a supportive community.

7. ***Multimedia Creation:*** Video Production and Editing: Children can create videos by recording, editing, and adding visual effects using video editing software. They can produce short films, music videos, or vlogs, expressing their ideas and creativity through visual storytelling.

8. ***Animation and Motion Graphics:*** Online animation tools and software allow children to create animated videos, cartoons, or motion graphics. They can bring characters and stories to life through animation, expressing their creativity dynamically and engagingly.

9. ***Online Communities and Collaborations:*** *Social Media Platforms:* Children can utilize social media platforms to share their creative works and connect with other young artists, writers, and musicians. They can engage in conversations, collaborate on projects, and find inspiration from a global creative community.

10. ***Collaborative Projects:*** Online platforms and forums offer opportunities for children to collaborate with others on creative projects. They can join forces with fellow young artists, writers, or musicians to create collaborative artworks, stories, or songs.

The internet provides various platforms and communities where children can express their creativity, receive feedback and support, and connect with like-minded individuals. It's important for parents and guardians to guide children in navigating these platforms safely and responsibly, ensuring they have positive and constructive experiences while expressing themselves creatively online.

Entertainment and Enrichment

Digital content has become increasingly accessible, providing children with a wide range of engaging and educational materials. Here's a discussion on the availability of digital content, such as games, videos, and interactive learning tools that entertain and educate children:

1. ***Educational Games and Apps:*** A vast selection of educational games and apps are designed to entertain children while promoting learning. These interactive experiences cover math, science, language, and problem-solving. They often incorporate engaging gameplay mechanics, rewards, and progress tracking to make learning enjoyable.

2. ***Video Content and Streaming Platforms:*** Video-sharing platforms like YouTube and streaming services offer children a wealth of educational and entertaining content. They can access various videos, including educational channels, documentaries, animated shows, and tutorials. These videos can spark curiosity, provide information, and enhance children's understanding of different topics.

3. ***Interactive Learning Tools and Websites:*** Numerous websites and platforms offer interactive learning tools and resources that engage children in hands-on learning experiences. These tools may include virtual labs, simulations, puzzles, and quizzes that facilitate active learning and make complex concepts more accessible and enjoyable.

4. ***E-books and Digital Libraries:*** Digital content has revolutionized the world of reading for children. E-books and digital libraries allow children to access a vast electronic collection of books and stories. Many platforms offer interactive features such as read-along narration, interactive illustrations, and educational games accompanying the reading experience.

5. ***Augmented Reality (AR) and Virtual Reality (VR):*** AR and VR technologies provide immersive and interactive experiences for children. They can explore virtual environments, historical sites, or scientific concepts, bringing learning to life in a unique and engaging way. AR and VR applications and platforms offer educational games, simulations, and virtual field trips that enhance children's understanding and captivate their attention.

6. ***Online Tutoring and Courses:*** Digital platforms provide opportunities for children to access online tutoring services

and courses. These platforms connect students with qualified tutors who offer personalized instruction and guidance. Children can learn independently, receive individualized feedback, and access resources tailored to their educational needs.

It's essential for parents and guardians to curate and monitor the digital content children engage with actively. They should prioritize age-appropriate, high-quality materials and encourage a healthy balance between entertainment and educational content. By leveraging the availability of digital content, children can be entertained, inspired, and empowered to explore and learn in interactive and engaging ways.

Section 2: Understanding the Risks

Online Predators and Grooming

While offering numerous benefits, the internet also poses potential dangers, particularly for individuals who may try to exploit children's vulnerabilities. Online grooming is a serious concern, wherein perpetrators build trust and manipulate children to engage them in sexual exploitation or other harmful activities. Parents, caregivers, and children must be aware of online grooming signs. Here are some key points to consider:

1. *Establishing Trust:* Groomers often work to gain children's trust by portraying themselves as friendly, understanding, and sympathetic individuals. They may use flattery, gifts, or attention to establish a bond with the child.

2. *Manipulative Techniques:* Groomers employ manipulative tactics to isolate the child and ensure compliance. They

may exploit the child's emotions, vulnerabilities, or curiosity, gradually pushing boundaries and making the child feel indebted or obligated.

3. ***Building Emotional Connections:*** Groomers aim to create emotional dependence by offering a sympathetic ear, understanding, and support. They may exploit the child's desire for attention, validation, or acceptance, gradually blurring boundaries between a genuine connection and manipulation.

4. ***Secrecy and Encouragement of Secrecy:*** Groomers often emphasize the need for secrecy, instructing children not to disclose their interactions to anyone, including parents or guardians. This secrecy is a red flag and a tactic to prevent intervention and detection.

5. ***Exploiting Curiosity and Sexual Content:*** Groomers may introduce sexual content, explicit conversations, or explicit materials to desensitize the child and blur boundaries. They may encourage the child to share personal information and photos or engage in explicit discussions.

6. ***Monitoring Online Activities:*** Groomers may closely monitor the child's online activities, including social media profiles, messaging apps, and interactions with others. They aim to exert control and manipulate the child's online behaviour.

To protect children from potential exploitation, it is important to recognize signs of online grooming by:

- Maintain open communication with children, ensuring they feel comfortable discussing their online experiences.

- Educate children about online safety, including the risks of online grooming and the importance of setting boundaries.

- Teach children to be cautious about sharing personal information or private conversations with strangers online.

- Encourage children to report suspicious or uncomfortable interactions to a trusted adult.

- Monitor children's online activities, including the platforms they use, the people they interact with, and any changes in their behaviour or emotional well-being.

- Use parental controls and privacy settings on devices and applications to enhance online safety.

- Stay informed about the latest trends, apps, and platforms children are using, and proactively engage in discussions about responsible online behaviour.

It's crucial for parents, caregivers, and educators to work together to create a safe and supportive online environment for children. By recognizing the signs of online grooming and taking proactive measures, we can help protect children from potential exploitation and ensure their online experiences are positive and secure.

Identify signs of online grooming and protect children from being exploited.

Children are vulnerable to individuals who seek to exploit them online. It is essential to be aware of the potential dangers and recognize signs of online grooming. Here are some important points to consider:

- *Manipulative and Deceptive Behavior:* Groomers may use manipulative tactics to gain a child's trust. They might pretend to be someone the child knows or shares common interests with. They often create a false sense of friendship and empathy to establish an emotional connection.

- *Building Trust and Isolation:* Groomers invest time in building trust and isolating the child from their family and friends. They may discourage the child from sharing their online interactions, creating a secret and exclusive relationship. This isolation makes it easier for the groomer to exert control.

- *Flattery and Gifts:* Groomers often shower children with excessive compliments, attention, and gifts. They exploit the child's desire for validation and use these tactics to manipulate and maintain control over them.

- *Sexualized Conversations:* One of the red flags of online grooming is the introduction of sexualized conversations or content. Groomers gradually steer conversations toward sexual topics, share explicit material, or ask the child for inappropriate images or videos. They may also try to normalize or justify such discussions to desensitize the child.

- *Emotional Manipulation:* Groomers manipulate children's emotions, playing on their vulnerabilities and insecurities. They may provide emotional support and act as a confidant, making the child feel dependent on their presence and approval.

- *Requesting Personal Information and Privacy Invasion:* Groomers often coax children into sharing personal information, such as their full name, address, school details, or family information. They may use this information to exploit or intimidate the child. Groomers might invade the child's privacy by demanding passwords or access to their social media accounts.

It is crucial to recognize signs of online grooming to protect children. Here are some potential grooming indicators:

- Sudden changes in behaviour, mood, or appearance, especially after spending time online.

- Increased secrecy regarding online activities and reluctance to share information or show messages.

- Excessive time spent online, especially during late hours of the night.

- Withdrawing from family and friends, especially those concerned about online activities.

- Receiving gifts, money, or packages from unknown sources.

- Displaying sexual knowledge or engaging in sexualized behaviours beyond their age level.

- Becoming emotionally attached to an online friend and prioritizing their opinions over others.

- Expressing fear, anxiety, or distress when unable to engage with a particular online contact.

If you notice any of these signs or suspect online grooming, it is crucial to take immediate action:

- Maintain open communication with the child and encourage them to share their online experiences.

- Document any suspicious interactions or conversations, including screenshots, and report them to appropriate authorities.

- Involve law enforcement or your local child protection agency, providing them with all relevant information.

- Block and report the groomer on the platform where the interaction occurs.

- Seek support from professionals, such as counsellors or therapists, specializing in child protection and online safety.

By being vigilant, educating children about online risks, and maintaining open lines of communication, we can protect children from potential exploitation and ensure their online safety.

Cyberbullying and Harassment

Cyberbullying is a significant issue in today's digital age and can harm a child's emotional well-being. It involves using digital technologies to harass, intimidate, or harm others. Here's a discussion on the prevalence of cyberbullying, its impact, and strategies for prevention and intervention:

1. *Prevalence of Cyberbullying:* Cyberbullying has become increasingly prevalent due to the widespread use of the internet and social media platforms. According to various studies, many children and teenagers have experienced some form of cyberbullying, ranging from hurtful comments and rumours to more severe forms of harassment and threats.

2. ***Impact on Emotional Well-being:*** Cyberbullying can severely affect a child's emotional well-being. It can lead to feelings of fear, anxiety, depression, and low self-esteem. Victims may experience social isolation, difficulty concentrating in school, and declining academic performance. In some cases, cyberbullying has even resulted in self-harm or suicide.

3. **Prevention Strategies:**

    - ***Education and Awareness:*** Promote awareness about cyberbullying among children, parents, and educators. Teach children about responsible digital citizenship, appropriate online behaviour, and the importance of empathy and respect toward others.

    - ***Establish Open Communication:*** Encourage children to talk openly about their online experiences. Create a supportive environment where they feel comfortable discussing any incidents of cyberbullying without fear of judgment or reprisal.

    - ***Digital Literacy and Safety Skills:*** Teach children about online safety, including privacy settings, reporting mechanisms, and the importance of not sharing personal information with strangers. Help them develop critical thinking skills to evaluate and respond to online content.

    - ***Positive Online Relationships:*** Foster positive online relationships by promoting kindness, empathy, and inclusivity. Encourage children to be supportive bystanders and intervene if they witness cyberbullying.

4. **Intervention Strategies:**

- ***Document and Report:*** Encourage children to save evidence of cyberbullying incidents, such as screenshots, messages, or emails. Report the incidents to relevant authorities or the platform where the bullying occurred.

- ***Block and Limit Contact:*** Advise children to block and avoid engaging with the cyberbully. Adjust privacy settings to limit the bully's access to personal information and restrict communication.

- ***Seek Support:*** Ensure that children have access to support systems, such as trusted adults, school counsellors, or helpline services. Encourage them to talk about their feelings and seek help when needed.

- ***Mental Health Support:*** If a child experiences significant emotional distress due to cyberbullying, consider seeking professional help from counsellors or therapists specializing in child and adolescent mental health.

- ***Collaboration with Schools and Communities:*** Establish partnerships with schools, community organizations, and online platforms to address cyberbullying effectively. Implement comprehensive anti-bullying policies and provide prevention, intervention, and support resources.

By focusing on prevention through education, fostering positive online behaviour, and providing appropriate intervention and support, we can mitigate the impact of cyberbullying and create a safer and more inclusive online environment for children.

Revenge porn

Online revenge porn, also known as non-consensual pornography or image-based abuse, refers to the act of sharing sexually explicit images or videos of a person without their consent, often intending to humiliate, harm, or harass them. This form of online harassment can have serious emotional, psychological, and even legal consequences for the victims. Dealing with revenge porn requires a multifaceted approach to protect victims, hold perpetrators accountable, and prevent further harm. Here's how to address online revenge porn:

1. **If You're a Victim:**

    - *Seek Emotional Support:* Reach out to friends, family, or professionals who can provide emotional support during this challenging time.

    - *Don't Respond:* Avoid engaging with the person who shared the content. Responding might escalate the situation or give them the attention they seek.

    - *Document Evidence:* Take screenshots, collect URLs, or save any information about the content and the person who shared it. This evidence might be useful for legal actions.

    - *Report to Platforms:* If the content is shared on social media, websites, or online forums, report it to the platform administrators. Many platforms have mechanisms for reporting explicit or abusive content.

    - *Contact Law Enforcement:* Contact local law enforcement if you believe a crime has been committed. Laws around revenge porn vary by jurisdiction, but many places have laws against this behaviour.

- ***Consult Legal Professionals:*** Seek legal advice from attorneys specializing in cybercrime, privacy, or internet law. They can guide you on potential legal actions you can take.

- ***Consider Takedown Requests:*** Some platforms, websites, and search engines allow you to submit requests for removing non-consensual explicit content.

2. **Preventive Measures:**

- **Educate Yourself:** Learn about online privacy, security, and the potential risks of sharing intimate content online.

- **Trust Wisely:** Be cautious about sharing intimate images or videos with anyone, even if you trust them. Once content is online, controlling its distribution cannot be easy.

- **Set Strong Privacy Settings:** On social media and other online platforms, adjust your privacy settings to control who can see your content.

- **Secure Your Devices:** Use strong passwords, two-factor authentication, and device security features to prevent unauthorized access to your content.

- **Communicate Boundaries:** If you're in a relationship, have open discussions about boundaries, consent, and the implications of sharing intimate content.

3. **Advocacy and Support:**

- *Support Organizations:* Seek assistance from organizations that specialize in supporting victims of online harassment, such as cyberbullying, revenge porn, and image-based abuse.

- *Advocate for Change:* Support advocacy efforts to strengthen laws against revenge porn and improve online safety measures.

Remember, dealing with revenge porn is emotionally challenging. Seek personal and legal support and take steps to protect your well-being while pursuing appropriate actions against those responsible.

Privacy and Data Security

Safeguarding personal information is paramount in the digital age, as sharing too much online can pose significant risks. Here's an address on the importance of protecting personal data and the risks associated with oversharing:

4. *Identity Theft and Fraud:* Sharing personal information online, such as full name, address, phone number, or date of birth, increases the risk of identity theft. Cybercriminals can misuse this information to impersonate individuals, commit financial fraud, or engage in other criminal activities. Safeguarding personal information helps protect against such risks.

5. *Online Predators and Grooming:* Sharing excessive personal information online can make children and teenagers vulnerable to online predators. Predators may use this information to manipulate, groom, or exploit individuals, risking their safety and well-being. Encouraging children to be cautious about sharing personal details is essential for their online safety.

6. ***Cyberbullying and Online Harassment:*** Oversharing personal information can make individuals more susceptible to cyberbullying and online harassment. Bullies can use this information to target and harm individuals, both emotionally and socially. Limiting personal information shared online reduces the chances of becoming a target.

7. ***Reputation and Digital Footprint:*** What is shared online can impact an individual's reputation and digital footprint. Inappropriate or personal information shared online can be accessed by others, potentially affecting future educational or career opportunities. Being mindful of the information shared helps maintain a positive online presence.

8. ***Privacy and Data Security:*** Safeguarding personal information is crucial for maintaining privacy and data security. Data breaches and unauthorized access to personal information can lead to identity theft, financial loss, or even exposure to sensitive personal details. Being cautious about sharing personal information helps protect privacy and minimize these risks

9. ***Social Engineering and Phishing Attacks:*** Cybercriminals often use personal information shared online to carry out social engineering attacks or phishing attempts. They may use the gathered information to craft convincing messages or impersonate trusted individuals, tricking individuals into disclosing more sensitive information or falling for scams.

To safeguard personal information and mitigate the associated risks:

- Be selective about the information shared online, especially on public platforms. Avoid sharing sensitive details like full addresses, phone numbers, social security numbers, or financial information.

- Adjust privacy settings on social media platforms and other online accounts to control who can access personal information and limit public visibility.

- Use strong and unique passwords for online accounts and enable two-factor authentication where available.

- Be cautious about sharing personal information in online conversations, emails, or messages, especially with unfamiliar individuals or unverified websites.

- Regularly review and update privacy settings on devices, applications, and online accounts to ensure maximum protection.

- Educate children about the importance of safeguarding personal information and the potential risks of oversharing online. Encourage them to seek guidance from trusted adults before sharing any personal details.

By being mindful of the information shared online and taking proactive measures to safeguard personal information, individuals can better protect their privacy, reduce the risks of online threats, and maintain a safer online presence.

Exposure to Inappropriate Content

The accessibility of age-inappropriate content is a significant challenge children face when using the internet. Exposure to such content can negatively affect their emotional well-being, cognitive development, and overall online safety. Here, we explore the challenges and strategies to mitigate the risk:

Challenges:

1. *Unfiltered Content:* The internet provides a vast amount of content, including explicit material, violence, hate speech,

and other age-inappropriate material. Children may encounter such content accidentally or intentionally while browsing or searching online.

2. ***Online Predators:*** Children may encounter individuals with malicious intentions who attempt to expose them to age-inappropriate content or engage in inappropriate conversations. These predators may exploit children's curiosity or lack of awareness to manipulate and groom them.

3. ***Peer Influence:*** Children may be influenced by their peers to explore and access age-inappropriate content. Peer pressure or a desire to fit in can lead them to seek out content unsuitable for their age or development stage.

Strategies to Mitigate the Risk

1. *Parental Supervision and Controls:*

   - Implement parental controls and filtering software to restrict access to age-inappropriate content.

   - Monitor children's online activities, including the websites they visit and the apps they use.

   - Set clear rules and guidelines for internet usage, including time limits and approved websites or platforms.

2. *Educating Children about Safe Internet Usage:*

   - Teach children about the potential risks and consequences of accessing age-inappropriate content.

   - Promote critical thinking skills and digital literacy, helping children evaluate the credibility and appropriateness of online content.

- Encourage open communication with children, fostering an environment where they feel comfortable discussing concerns or encounters with inappropriate content.

3. **Establishing Trustworthy Online Sources:**

- Introduce children to reliable and age-appropriate websites, search engines, and online resources for educational and entertainment needs.

- Teach them how to identify reputable sources of information and encourage them to seek guidance when encountering unfamiliar content.

4. **Safe Browsing Practices:**

- Teach children how to use safe search filters and enable restricted modes on search engines and content platforms.

- Encourage them to bookmark and use trusted websites and avoid clicking on suspicious links or pop-ups.

5. **Digital Citizenship and Responsible Online Behavior:**

- Educate children about ethical online behaviour, respect for others, and the importance of avoiding and reporting inappropriate content.

- Teach them about the potential consequences of sharing or forwarding age-inappropriate content and the impact it can have on themselves and others.

6. **Building Resilience and Coping Skills:**

- Foster resilience in children by teaching them how to manage their emotions and handle disturbing or inappropriate content they may come across online.

- Provide guidance on coping strategies, such as closing the browser window, talking to a trusted adult, or reporting the content to appropriate authorities.

It is crucial to have a multi-layered approach involving parental guidance, education, and technological tools to mitigate the risk of children accessing or being exposed to age-inappropriate content. By implementing these strategies, we can create a safer online environment for children and help them navigate the digital world responsibly.

Online Scams and Fraud

Online scams often target children due to their vulnerability and lack of awareness about such fraudulent activities. Educating children about common online scams and how to recognize and avoid them is essential. Here are some common online scams targeting children and strategies to educate kids about them:

1. *Phishing Scams:*

- Explain to children what phishing is and how scammers use deceptive emails, messages, or websites to trick them into revealing personal information.

- Teach them not to click on suspicious links or download attachments from unknown sources.

- Encourage them to verify the authenticity of emails or messages by contacting the organization or person using trusted contact information.

2. *Fake Social Media Accounts and Friend Requests:*

- Make children aware that scammers may create fake social media accounts to impersonate friends, celebrities, or trusted individuals.

- Teach them to be cautious when accepting friend requests from unknown individuals and to verify the identity of people they interact with online.

- Encourage them to report suspicious accounts or activities to the social media platform.

3. *Online Shopping Scams:*

- Explain to children the risks associated with online shopping, including counterfeit products, fake websites, and payment fraud.

- Teach them only to make online purchases from trusted and reputable websites.

- Emphasize the importance of not sharing personal or financial information with unknown or unverified online sellers.

4. *In-App Purchases and Microtransactions:*

- Educate children about the potential risks of in-app purchases and microtransactions in games and apps.

- Teach them to be cautious when prompted to make purchases within apps and to seek parental permission before making any transactions.

- Set clear guidelines and restrictions on in-app purchases and ensure children understand the financial implications.

5. *Prize or Sweepstakes Scams:*

- Explain to children that legitimate sweepstakes or contests do not require payment or personal information upfront.

- Teach them to be skeptical of unsolicited messages or emails claiming they have won a prize or sweepstakes.

- Encourage them to consult a trusted adult before providing personal information or making payments.

6. *Online Gaming Scams:*

- Educate children about scams that target online gaming platforms, such as fraudulent game codes, fake virtual items, or phishing attempts through in-game messages.

- Teach them to be cautious when trading or purchasing virtual items and to use trusted platforms or official game stores.

- Emphasize the importance of not sharing game account credentials with anyone and using strong, unique passwords.

7. *Donation Scams:*

- Teach children about the importance of verifying the legitimacy of charitable organizations before making donations.

- Encourage them to seek guidance from a trusted adult when they want to donate money or support a cause online.

Regularly discussing online scams and reinforcing these strategies will help children develop critical thinking skills, skepticism, and a healthy level of caution while navigating the digital world. Additionally, setting clear guidelines on online activities and supervising their online interactions can provide an added layer of protection.

Inform parents about common online scams targeting children and how to educate kids to recognize and avoid them.

Section 3: Digital Citizenship and Responsible Behaviour

Digital Footprint and Online Reputation

Children's digital footprints refer to the trail of information and data they leave behind while engaging in online activities. This digital footprint can have a lasting impact on their online reputation and future opportunities. Here, we discuss the significance of children's digital footprints and the importance of cultivating a positive online reputation:

1. *Permanence of Online Information:* Anything children share or post online, including photos, comments, and social media activity, can become a permanent part of their

digital footprint. This information can be accessed, stored, and potentially used by others years later. It is crucial for children to understand that their online actions can have long-term consequences.

2. ***Impact on Personal and Professional Opportunities:*** A positive online reputation can open doors to future personal and professional opportunities. Employers, college admissions officers, and scholarship committees often research applicants' online presence to gain insight into their character, values, and judgment. A negative digital footprint can hinder these opportunities.

3. ***Building Trust and Credibility:*** A positive online reputation helps children build trust and credibility among their peers, teachers, and other online communities. Children can establish themselves as reliable and trustworthy individuals in the digital space by consistently demonstrating responsible online behaviour, respectful communication, and meaningful contributions.

4. ***Protecting Personal Privacy and Safety:*** Cultivating a positive online reputation involves being mindful of the personal information shared and the privacy settings utilized. To protect their privacy and safety, children should understand the importance of safeguarding their personal information, such as addresses, phone numbers, and sensitive details.

5. ***Digital Citizenship and Ethical Behavior:*** Promoting a positive online reputation encourages children to become responsible digital citizens. They learn to respect others' privacy, refrain from cyberbullying or online harassment, and contribute positively to online communities.

Cultivating ethical behaviour online fosters a healthy and inclusive digital environment for everyone.

Strategies to Cultivate a Positive Online Reputation

1. *Educate on Digital Permanence:* Teach children about the permanence of online information and how it can impact their future. Encourage them to think before posting and consider their online actions' potential consequences.

2. *Set Guidelines and Monitor Online Activity:* Establish clear guidelines for online behaviour and discuss expectations with children. Regularly monitor their online activities to ensure they are adhering to these guidelines.

3. *Foster Digital Literacy and Critical Thinking:* Help children develop digital literacy skills, including evaluating online content for accuracy and reliability. Encourage critical thinking when interacting with others online and promote respectful communication.

4. *Encourage Positive Online Contributions:* Encourage children to engage in positive online activities, such as sharing their knowledge, participating in meaningful discussions, or supporting causes they care about. Foster their creativity and help them positively showcase their talents and interests.

5. *Lead by Example:* Be a positive role model by demonstrating responsible online behaviour and practicing good digital citizenship. Children often learn from observing their parents or guardians, so exemplify the values you want them to adopt.

6. *Regular Conversations and Open Communication:* Maintain open lines of communication with children about

their online experiences. Encourage them to share any concerns or issues they encounter and provide guidance and support when needed.

By guiding children to cultivate a positive online reputation, we empower them to navigate the digital world responsibly, make informed choices, and create a digital footprint that reflects their values, achievements, and potential.

Ethical Behavior and Respect

Promoting kindness, respect, and ethical behaviour in online interactions is crucial for fostering a positive and inclusive digital environment. Here, we emphasize the impact of words and actions and the importance of upholding these values online:

1. *The Power of Words:*

    - Teach children that words have the power to uplift, inspire, and bring joy to others, but they can also hurt, demean, and cause harm.

    - Emphasize the importance of choosing words carefully and considering their impact on others before posting or commenting online.

    - Encourage children to use their words to spread kindness, support, and positivity in their online interactions.

2. *Respectful Communication:*

    - Instill in children the value of treating others with respect, regardless of their differences or opinions.

    - Teach them to engage in constructive discussions, listen to different perspectives, and express their thoughts and disagreements in a respectful and considerate manner.

- Encourage empathy and help children understand the potential impact of their words on others' feelings and experiences.

3. *Digital Empathy:*

- Foster digital empathy by helping children understand that there are real people with real emotions behind the screens.

- Encourage them to think about how others may perceive their words or actions and how they would feel if they were in the other person's shoes.

- Teach them to be mindful of the potential consequences of their online behaviour and its lasting impact on individuals' well-being.

4. *Responsible Sharing:*

- Teach children to be responsible and ethical when sharing content online.

- Emphasize the importance of respecting copyright laws, giving credit to original creators, and obtaining permission before sharing others' work.

- Help them understand the implications of sharing personal information, photos, or videos without consent and the potential risks it can pose.

5. *Positive Online Influence:*

- Encourage children to use their online presence as a force for good and to be positive influencers in their digital communities.

- Inspire them to share content that promotes kindness, inclusivity, creativity, and knowledge.

- Help them recognize the impact they can have in shaping a positive and supportive online environment.

6. *Reporting and Intervening:*

- Teach children to recognize and report any instances of online harassment, cyberbullying, or unethical behaviour they come across.

- Encourage them to stand up against such behaviour and support those who are being targeted.

- Promote the idea that reporting and intervening can help create a safer and more respectful online space for everyone.

By promoting these values of kindness, respect, and ethical behaviour in online interactions, we empower children to become responsible digital citizens who contribute positively to the digital world. It is essential to emphasize that our words and actions online have real-life consequences and that we can positively impact others through our online behaviour.

Media Literacy and Critical Thinking

Developing critical thinking skills in children is crucial for navigating the vast amount of information available online and distinguishing between reliable and unreliable sources. Here are some strategies to help children cultivate their critical thinking skills:

1. ***Teach Source Evaluation:***

   - Teach children to evaluate the credibility and reliability of online sources by considering factors such as author expertise, publisher reputation, and evidence-based information.

   - Encourage them to look for authoritative sources such as educational institutions, government websites, reputable news organizations, or peer-reviewed publications.

   - Discuss the importance of cross-referencing information from multiple sources to ensure accuracy.

2. ***Questioning and Verifying Information:***

   - Teach children to ask critical questions about the information they encounter online, such as:

      ➢ Who is the author? What are their qualifications and expertise?

      ➢ What evidence or sources support the claims made?

      ➢ Is the information presented in a balanced and unbiased manner?

      ➢ Are there any red flags, such as overly sensational language or extreme claims?

- Guide them in verifying information by fact-checking through trusted fact-checking websites or referring to reliable sources for confirmation.

3. *Analyzing Bias and Perspective:*

- Help children understand the concept of bias and how it can influence the presentation of information.

- Encourage them to identify potential biases in online content, such as political, commercial, or cultural biases.

- Teach them to seek out diverse perspectives and consider different viewpoints before forming opinions or drawing conclusions.

4. *Developing Media Literacy Skills:*

- Teach children to analyze different media types, including articles, images, videos, and social media posts.

- Help them recognize potential manipulations, such as photo editing or selective presentation of information.

- Discuss the influence of advertising and sponsored content and the need to approach such content with skepticism.

5. *Identifying Reliable Websites and Sources:*

- Provide children with a list of reliable and age-appropriate websites and resources for their research and learning.

- Guide them in using search engines effectively, including using advanced search features and applying filters to find accurate and relevant information.

6. *Encouraging Independent Thinking:*

    - Encourage children to think independently and develop their own opinions based on evidence and critical analysis.

    - Foster an environment where they feel comfortable questioning information and engaging in respectful debates.

7. *Open Dialogue and Guidance:*

    - Maintain open lines of communication with children, allowing them to discuss their online experiences, questions, and concerns.

    - Be available to provide guidance and support in navigating complex or confusing online information.

By fostering critical thinking skills in children, we equip them with the tools needed to evaluate online information effectively, make informed decisions, and confidently navigate the digital landscape. Through practice and guidance, children can develop a discerning approach to online content and become empowered consumers and creators of information.

Section 4: Balancing Online and Offline Life

Digital Addiction and Screen Time Management

Excessive screen time can pose various risks to children's physical and mental well-being, including sedentary behaviour, sleep disturbances, decreased social interaction, and reduced academic performance. Setting healthy boundaries around screen time is essential. Here are some strategies to help parents establish these boundaries:

1. *Define Clear Screen Time Guidelines:*

    - Set clear rules and expectations regarding screen time duration and specific activities allowed.

    - Discuss these guidelines with your children, explaining the reasons behind them and the importance of balance in their overall well-being.

2. *Lead by Example:*

    - Model healthy screen time behaviour by demonstrating responsible and limited device use.

    - Engage in alternative activities such as reading, outdoor play, or family interactions that do not involve screens.

3. *Create Screen-Free Zones and Times:*

    - Designate specific areas in the house, such as bedrooms or mealtime areas, as screen-free zones.

    - Establish screen-free times, such as during family meals or before bedtime, to encourage face-to-face interactions and quality time together.

4. *Encourage Physical Activity and Outdoor Play:*

- Emphasize the importance of physical activity and outdoor play for children's overall health and development.

- Set aside daily dedicated time for exercise, sports, or other outdoor activities to reduce sedentary screen time.

5. **Foster Offline Hobbies and Interests:**

- Encourage children to explore and develop offline hobbies, such as reading, drawing, playing musical instruments, or engaging in sports.

- Provide access to age-appropriate books, art supplies, musical instruments, or other materials that support their interests.

6. **Establish Tech-Free Bedtime Routine:**

- Avoid screen time at least an hour before bedtime to ensure better quality sleep.

- Encourage relaxing activities before bed, such as reading a book or calming conversation, to promote better sleep hygiene.

7. **Use Parental Control and Screen Time Management Tools:**

- Utilize parental control features available on devices or use third-party apps to set time limits, monitor usage, and block access to inappropriate content.

- Set up device-free zones or charging stations outside of bedrooms to limit access during specific times.

8. *Encourage Balanced Online Activities:*

- Encourage children to engage in educational and productive online activities, such as educational apps, creative platforms, or learning websites.

- Guide them to explore online content that enhances their knowledge, skills, and interests.

9. *Promote Social Interactions and Family Bonding:*

- Encourage children to engage in face-to-face interactions, spend time with friends, and participate in social activities.

- Plan family activities, outings, or game nights that promote bonding and reduce reliance on screen-based entertainment.

10. *Maintain Open Communication:*

- Keep an open dialogue with your children about their online activities, concerns, and experiences.

- Regularly discuss the importance of balance, responsible screen use, and the potential risks of excessive screen time.

Every child is different, so it's important to tailor screen time boundaries to their age, developmental stage, and individual needs. By setting healthy boundaries and promoting a balanced approach to screen time, parents can help children develop a healthy relationship with technology while prioritizing their overall well-being.

Promoting Offline Activities and Social Interactions

Maintaining a balanced lifestyle incorporating offline activities, face-to-face interactions, and physical exercise is essential for children's overall well-being and healthy development. Here are some key reasons to highlight the importance of balance:

1. **Physical Health:**

    *   Engaging in offline activities and physical exercise helps children maintain healthy body weight, develop motor skills, and improve cardiovascular fitness.

    *   Regular exercise strengthens muscles and bones, enhances coordination and balance, and reduces the risk of obesity and related health issues.

2. **Mental and Emotional Well-being:**

    *   Balancing offline activities fosters mental and emotional well-being by providing opportunities for relaxation, stress reduction, and improved mood.

    *   Face-to-face interactions with family, friends, and peers offer social support, strengthen relationships, and promote a sense of belonging and connection.

3. **Cognitive Development:**

    *   Offline activities, such as reading, creative play, and problem-solving games, stimulate cognitive development, imagination, and critical thinking skills.

    *   Face-to-face interactions enhance communication, social skills, empathy, and emotional intelligence.

4. **Creativity and Imagination:**

- Engaging in offline activities, such as art, crafts, music, or imaginative play, nurtures creativity, self-expression, and innovation.

- Unplugging from screens allows children's minds to wander, explore new ideas, and develop their unique talents and interests.

5. *Healthy Relationships:*

- Face-to-face interactions allow children to develop and maintain healthy relationships, practice empathy, resolve conflicts, and build social skills.

- Physical presence and non-verbal communication cues play a vital role in understanding others' emotions, fostering deeper connections, and developing meaningful friendships.

6. *Balance and Time Management:*

- Encouraging a balanced lifestyle helps children develop time management skills and establish healthy habits early on.

- By allocating time for various activities, children learn to prioritize their responsibilities, manage their schedules, and make informed choices about how they spend their time.

7. *Self-Reflection and Mindfulness:*

- Offline activities and quiet moments provide children with self-reflection, introspection, and mindfulness opportunities.

- Disconnecting from screens allows children to be present at the moment, focus on their thoughts and feelings, and develop a deeper understanding of themselves.

8. *Exposure to the Natural World:*

- Encouraging outdoor activities and physical exercise exposes children to nature, fresh air, and sunlight, which benefits their physical and mental health.

- Exploring the natural world promotes curiosity, environmental awareness, and a sense of stewardship for the planet.

Children can develop holistically by maintaining a balanced lifestyle that includes offline activities, face-to-face interactions, and physical exercise, cultivating their physical, mental, social, and emotional well-being. It is important to provide a variety of experiences that allow children to thrive both online and offline, fostering a healthy and well-rounded approach to life.

Understanding the digital world's benefits, risks, and challenges is essential for parents as they navigate their children's online experiences. Parents can guide their children toward responsible and safe digital engagement by recognizing the advantages and being aware of potential risks. By fostering a healthy digital environment and promoting good digital citizenship, parents can empower their children to make informed decisions and maximize the benefits of the digital world while mitigating the associated risks.

CHAPTER 2: BUILDING A FOUNDATION OF DIGITAL LITERACY

Section 1: Understanding how data and digital behaviour work

Online risks and responsible digital behaviour

Teaching children about online risks and responsible digital behaviour is crucial in today's digital age. Here are some key points to consider when educating children about these topics:

1. ***Open communication:*** Establish an open and honest line of communication with children regarding their online activities. Encourage them to ask questions, share their experiences, and express any concerns they may have. Create a supportive environment where they feel comfortable discussing online risks.

2. ***Online privacy:*** Teach children the importance of safeguarding their personal information online. Explain what information should not be shared, such as full name, address, phone number, school details, and passwords. Emphasize that they should only share personal information with trusted individuals and platforms.

3. ***Cyberbullying awareness:*** Discuss the issue of cyberbullying and its impact on individuals. Teach children about the different forms of cyberbullying, such as harassment, spreading rumours, or posting hurtful comments or images. Encourage them to be kind and

respectful online and report any cyberbullying they witness or experience.

4. *Identifying scams and phishing:* Educate children about online scams and phishing attempts. Teach them how to recognize suspicious emails, messages, or websites that may try to steal personal information or money. Encourage them to be cautious and verify the authenticity of any requests for personal information or financial transactions.

5. *Digital footprint:* Help children understand that their online activities leave a digital footprint that can have long-term consequences. Discuss the potential impact of their online behaviour on future education, career opportunities, and personal relationships. Encourage them to think before posting or sharing anything online.

6. *Online friendships and strangers:* Teach children about the risks associated with interacting with strangers online. Emphasize the importance of not sharing personal information or meeting up with individuals they have only met online. Encourage them only to accept friend requests or communicate with people they know in real life.

7. *Critical thinking and media literacy:* Develop children's critical thinking skills to help them evaluate the credibility of online information and media. Teach them to question the source, check for multiple perspectives, and look for evidence before believing or sharing information. Encourage them to be responsible digital citizens who promote accurate and reliable content.

8. *Digital balance and well-being:* Discuss the importance of maintaining a healthy balance between online and offline activities. Encourage children to limit screen time, engage

in physical activities, pursue hobbies, and spend time with family and friends offline. Teach them to recognize signs of online addiction or negative impacts on their mental health.

9. ***Online security practices:*** Teach children the importance of using strong and unique passwords for different online accounts. Explain the concept of two-factor authentication (2FA) and the benefits of enabling it for added security. Encourage them to update their devices, apps, and software to protect against vulnerabilities.

10. ***Reporting and seeking help:*** Teach children how to report inappropriate or harmful content or behaviour on different online platforms. Make them aware of trusted adult figures they can turn to, such as parents, teachers, or school counsellors if they encounter troubling situations or need guidance.

Teaching children about online risks and responsible digital behaviour is an ongoing process. Stay informed about current trends and technologies, adapt your guidance accordingly, and regularly engage in conversations about online safety.

Section 2: Importance of Trust and Open Communication

Establishing open communication and trust

Establishing open communication and trust with kids about their online activity is essential for their safety and well-being. Here are some strategies to foster open communication and build trust:

1. ***Start early:*** Start the conversation about online activity and responsible digital behaviour as soon as possible. As soon as kids start using digital devices or accessing the internet, introduce age-appropriate discussions about online safety and responsible online behaviour.

2. ***Be approachable:*** Create an environment where children feel comfortable coming to you with questions or concerns about their online experiences. Be open-minded, non-judgmental, and responsive when they seek guidance. Avoid overreacting or punishing them for honest mistakes, as this may discourage open communication in the future.

3. ***Active listening:*** Practice listening when your child talks about their online experiences. Give them your undivided attention, maintain eye contact, and show genuine interest in what they have to say. Reflect on their feelings and concerns to demonstrate that you understand and empathize with their experiences.

4. ***Non-blaming approach:*** Avoid blaming or shaming children for their online activities or mistakes. Instead, focus on guiding them toward making better choices and learning from their experiences. Encourage them to discuss any challenges they encounter and offer support and solutions without judgment.

5. ***Stay informed:*** Stay updated on current trends, popular apps, and children's websites. This will help you understand their online world better and engage in meaningful conversations about their digital experiences. Research and familiarize yourself with the potential risks and challenges they may face online.

6. ***Set clear expectations:*** Establish clear rules and expectations regarding online behaviour, screen time limits, and the types of content they can access. Involve children in creating these rules to ensure they understand and take ownership of them. Regularly revisit and revise the rules as necessary.

7. ***Educate together:*** Explore the online world with your child. Watch videos, read articles, and discuss online safety and responsible digital behaviour together. Use age-appropriate resources and interactive activities to enhance their understanding. This collaborative approach helps build trust and reinforces your role as a supportive guide.

8. ***Encourage questions:*** Encourage your child to ask questions about online safety and responsible behaviour. Provide honest and age-appropriate answers, and if you don't know something, research the topic together to find accurate information. Foster an environment where curiosity is encouraged, and no question is considered silly or irrelevant.

9. ***Be a role model:*** Set a positive example by practicing responsible digital behaviour yourself. Children often imitate their parents' actions, demonstrating good online habits, such as protecting their privacy, using technology mindfully, and treating others respectfully in online interactions.

10. ***Address challenges together:*** If your child encounters a problem or faces an online risk, approach it as a team. Work together to find solutions, report any necessary incidents, and emphasize that they can rely on you for support. Reinforce that mistakes happen, and the important

thing is to learn from them and make better choices in the future.

Remember, building trust takes time and consistency. By establishing open communication, being supportive, and actively engaging with your child's online experiences, you can create a safe and trusting environment where they feel comfortable discussing their digital lives with you.

Promoting critical thinking and media literacy skills

Fostering critical thinking and media literacy skills for kids online is crucial in helping them navigate the vast amount of information they encounter online. Here are some strategies to encourage and develop these skills:

1. *Teach source evaluation:* Help children understand the importance of evaluating the credibility and reliability of online sources. Teach them to question the source of information, check for author expertise, examine biases, and look for corroborating evidence from multiple reliable sources.

2. *Discuss misinformation and fake news:* Explain to children that not everything they see online is true. Discuss misinformation and phony news examples, highlighting the potential consequences of believing and spreading false information. Encourage them to verify information through fact-checking websites or trusted sources before accepting it as true.

3. *Explore different perspectives:* Encourage children to seek out and consider different perspectives on a given topic. Teach them to recognize and appreciate diverse viewpoints and understand that critical thinking involves considering multiple sides of an issue before forming an opinion.

4. ***Analyze media techniques:*** Help children understand the persuasive techniques used in media, such as emotional appeals, sensationalism, or cherry-picking information. Teach them to recognize these techniques and question the motives behind the content they encounter online.

5. ***Encourage fact-checking:*** Teach children how to fact-check information online. Show them reliable fact-checking websites or tools they can use to verify claims, such as Snopes, FactCheck.org, or Google's Fact Check Explorer. Encourage them to cross-reference information from multiple credible sources.

6. ***Develop critical questioning skills:*** Teach children to ask critical questions about the content they consume online. Encourage them to ask who created the content, its purpose, and whether it is backed by evidence or reliable sources. Instill in them a curiosity to dig deeper and seek more information before accepting information at face value.

7. ***Discuss bias and objectivity:*** Help children understand the concept of bias in media. Discuss how different factors, such as personal beliefs, political affiliations, or financial interests, can influence the presentation of information. Encourage them to identify and consider biases when evaluating the credibility and objectivity of sources.

8. ***Engage in media literacy activities:*** Incorporate media literacy activities into your child's learning experience. This can include analyzing news articles, advertisements, or social media posts and discussing their credibility and possible biases. Encourage them to create their own media content, such as videos or blogs, focusing on accuracy, fairness, and responsible sharing.

9. *Foster healthy skepticism:* Encourage children to be skeptically minded but not cynical. Teach them to question information without automatically dismissing it and to seek evidence and reliable sources to support or refute claims. Foster a balance between critical thinking and maintaining an open mind.

10. *Be a guide and discuss real-world examples:* Discuss current events, controversial topics, or viral online stories with your child. Help them critically analyze these examples, identify potential biases, and evaluate the credibility of the information presented. Use these opportunities to reinforce media literacy skills and promote thoughtful discussions.

Promoting critical thinking and media literacy skills empowers children to navigate the online world more effectively, make informed decisions, and become responsible digital content consumers and creators. These skills are essential for them to be discerning, thoughtful, and responsible digital citizens.

CHAPTER 3: FORTIFYING ONLINE PRIVACY

Section 1: Understanding the Data on Your System

Safeguarding personal information and sensitive data

Safeguarding kids' personal information and sensitive data online is crucial to protect their privacy and safety. Here are some important measures you can take:

1. ***Educate children about online privacy:*** Teach kids about the importance of keeping personal information private. Help them understand what information should not be shared online, such as full names, addresses, phone numbers, school names, or passwords.

2. ***Use strong and unique passwords:*** Encourage children to create strong and unique passwords for their online accounts. Emphasize the importance of not sharing passwords with anyone, including friends.

3. ***Enable privacy settings:*** Ensure privacy settings are enabled on social media platforms, online games, and other websites your children use. Adjust the settings to restrict the sharing of personal information and limit who can view their profiles or access their data.

4. ***Monitor online activities:*** Keep an eye on your child's online activities and establish open lines of communication. Encourage them to talk to you if they encounter suspicious or uncomfortable situations online.

5. ***Teach responsible social media use:*** Guide children on responsible social media use, including being cautious about accepting friend requests or following people they don't know personally. Discuss the potential risks of sharing personal information or posting sensitive content online.

6. ***Install parental control software:*** Consider installing parental control software or using built-in parental control features on devices to filter and block inappropriate content, set time limits, and monitor online activities.

7. ***Be aware of online scams and phishing:*** Educate your children about common online scams and phishing attempts. Teach them to be skeptical of suspicious emails, messages, or requests for personal information.

8. ***Regularly update software and devices:*** Keep software, operating systems, and security applications up to date on your child's devices to ensure they have the latest security patches and protections against vulnerabilities.

9. ***Encourage safe browsing habits:*** Teach children to use safe browsing habits, such as avoiding clicking on unknown links or downloading files from untrusted sources. Use child-friendly search engines or enable safe search filters to reduce exposure to inappropriate content.

10. ***Foster open communication:*** Create a safe and non-judgmental environment where children feel comfortable discussing their online experiences and concerns. Encourage them to approach you if they encounter any online threats, cyberbullying, or harassment.

Remember, effective protection requires a combination of parental guidance, education, and appropriate tools and technologies.

Regularly discuss online safety with your children and adapt the strategies as they grow and face new challenges in the digital world.

Section 2: Advantages of a Secure Setup

Understanding privacy settings on devices, apps, and social media platforms

Understanding privacy settings on devices, apps, and social media platforms is crucial for safeguarding kids' online privacy. Here are some key areas to focus on:

1. **Devices:**

    - *Device Passcode:* Set a strong passcode on your child's device to prevent unauthorized access.

    - *Biometric Authentication:* Enable fingerprint or face recognition as an additional security measure.

    - *App Permissions:* Review and manage app permissions to control access to features like location, camera, microphone, contacts, and photos. Disable unnecessary permissions for apps that don't require them.

2. **Operating Systems:**

    - *Privacy Settings:* Explore the privacy settings on the operating system to customize privacy options, such as location sharing, advertising tracking, app permissions, and data collection.

    - *Restriction Controls:* Utilize built-in parental control features to set restrictions on app downloads, in-app purchases, and access to certain content or features.

3. **Social Media Platforms:**

- *Privacy Policies:* Familiarize yourself with the privacy policies of social media platforms your child uses to understand how their data is collected, stored, and shared.

- *Account Privacy Settings:* Adjust account privacy settings to limit who can view your child's profile, posts, and personal information. Enable features like private profiles and approval for friend requests.

- *Location Sharing:* Disable location sharing or limit it to trusted friends only.

- *Tagging and Mentions:* Manage tagging and mentions settings to control who can tag or mention your child in posts or photos.

- *Blocking and Reporting:* Teach your child how to block or report any accounts that engage in inappropriate or harmful behaviour.

4. **Messaging and Communication Apps:**

- *Encrypted Messaging:* Use messaging apps that offer end-to-end encryption to protect the privacy of your child's conversations.

- *Privacy Settings:* Explore the privacy settings in messaging apps to control who can contact your child and who can see their online status.

- *Group Chats:* Review group chat settings and encourage your child to only participate in groups with trusted individuals.

5. **Parental Control Apps and Software:**

   - *Content Filtering:* Install parental control apps or software that provide content filtering to block inappropriate websites, apps, or search results.

   - *Screen Time Management:* Utilize features that allow you to set time limits for device usage and establish schedules for when devices can be used.

   - *Activity Monitoring:* Some parental control apps offer activity monitoring features, allowing you to track your child's online activities and receive alerts for concerning behaviour.

Regularly review and update privacy settings as new features are introduced or platforms change their policies. It's also essential to have open conversations with your child about the importance of privacy and responsible online behaviour. Encourage them to ask questions and seek your guidance when navigating privacy settings or encountering unfamiliar situations online.

Eeducating children about the importance of privacy protection

Educating children about the importance of privacy protection is crucial in helping them develop safe and responsible online habits. Here are some key points to consider when teaching kids about privacy protection:

1. ***Define personal information:*** Start by explaining what personal information is, such as full name, address, phone number, school name, email address, and passwords. Help

children understand that this information should be kept private and not shared with strangers online.

2. ***Discuss online risks:*** Have age-appropriate conversations about the potential dangers of sharing personal information online. Talk about the importance of protecting their privacy to prevent identity theft, scams, cyberbullying, and other forms of online harassment.

3. ***Emphasize the permanence of online sharing:*** Help children understand that information shared online can stay there indefinitely, even if they delete it later. Teach them to think before posting, considering the potential consequences and impact on their privacy and reputation.

4. ***Teach responsible social media use:*** Guide children on responsible use of social media platforms. Discuss the importance of adjusting privacy settings, approving friend requests from known individuals only, and being cautious about sharing personal information or posting sensitive content.

5. ***Recognize and avoid online scams:*** Educate children about common online scams, such as phishing emails, suspicious links, or requests for personal information. Teach them to be skeptical and avoid sharing information or clicking on links unless they are certain about the legitimacy of the request.

6. ***Encourage password security:*** Teach children the importance of creating strong, unique passwords and not sharing them with anyone. Emphasize the need to use a combination of letters, numbers, and symbols and to change passwords regularly.

7. ***Discuss the concept of consent:*** Teach children the importance of obtaining consent before sharing someone else's personal information or posting their pictures online. Help them understand the importance of respecting others' privacy.

8. ***Online reputation management:*** Explain to children how their online actions can shape their reputation. Teach them to think about the potential impact of their posts and comments on how others perceive them.

9. ***Encourage open communication:*** Create an environment where children feel comfortable discussing their online experiences and concerns. Encourage them to approach you if they encounter suspicious or uncomfortable situations online.

10. ***Be a role model:*** Children learn by observing, so set a good example by practicing privacy protection yourself. Demonstrate responsible online behaviour, respect others' privacy, and involve your child in discussions about privacy and security measures you take as a family.

Remember that ongoing communication, reinforcement, and age-appropriate conversations ensure children understand and prioritize online privacy. Encourage them to ask questions, seek guidance, and discuss any concerns they may have as they navigate the digital world.

CHAPTER 4: NAVIGATING SOCIAL MEDIA SAFELY

Section 1: Tips for Staying Safe in the Digital Age

The risks and benefits of social media for children

Social media has become an integral part of our lives, including those of children. While there are certain benefits associated with social media use, it is important to be aware of the risks and challenges it can pose to children. Here are some of the risks and benefits of social media for children:

Dangers of social media for children:

1. *Cyberbullying:* Social media platforms can be breeding grounds for cyberbullying, where children may face harassment, humiliation, or threats from peers. This can lead to emotional distress, anxiety, and even depression.

2. *Online predators:* Children may unknowingly come into contact with individuals who have malicious intentions, such as sexual predators. They can use social media platforms to groom children, posing a risk to their safety.

3. *Privacy concerns:* Children may inadvertently share personal information online, compromising their privacy and exposing them to potential risks. They might not fully understand the implications of sharing personal details publicly.

4. *Mental health issues:* Excessive use of social media can contribute to feelings of inadequacy, low self-esteem, and social comparison. It can also lead to addictive behaviours and negatively impact a child's mental well-being.

5. *Inappropriate content:* Children may be exposed to age-inappropriate content, including violence, explicit language, or graphic imagery, which can have a detrimental effect on their emotional and psychological development.

Benefits of social media for children:

1. *Social connections:* Social media platforms can help children connect and communicate with friends, family, and peers. It can provide a sense of belonging and facilitate social interaction, especially for those who may be geographically separated.

2. *Educational opportunities:* Social media can be a valuable tool for learning, with access to educational resources, tutorials, and online communities that promote knowledge sharing and skill development.

3. *Creativity and self-expression:* Social media platforms can be channels for children to express their creativity, share their artwork, writing, or music, and receive feedback and encouragement from others.

4. *Cultural awareness:* Social media enables children to engage worldwide with diverse cultures, traditions, and perspectives. It can foster empathy, understanding, and global awareness.

5. *Networking and career opportunities:* As children grow older, social media can help them build professional

networks, explore career opportunities, and connect with mentors or experts in their areas of interest.

It is essential for parents and guardians to guide children's social media use and ensure their safety online. This can be done through open communication, setting appropriate boundaries, teaching digital literacy skills, and encouraging responsible online behaviour.

Creating and managing safe social media profiles

Creating and managing safe social media profiles for children is crucial to protect their privacy, ensure their online safety, and mitigate potential risks. Here are some tips to help create and manage safe social media profiles for children:

1. *Age-appropriate platforms:* Choose social media platforms suitable for your child's age group. Many platforms have minimum age requirements, and it's important to abide by them to ensure a safer online environment.

2. *Privacy settings:* Familiarize yourself with the privacy settings of the chosen social media platforms. Adjust the settings to restrict access to your child's profile and content, limiting it to trusted friends and family members.

3. *Strong passwords:* Create strong and unique passwords for your child's social media accounts. Encourage them to use a combination of letters, numbers, and symbols and avoid using personal information in passwords.

4. *Limited personal information:* Teach your child to be cautious about sharing personal information on their social media profiles. This includes their full name, address, phone number, school name, and other identifiable details.

Emphasize the importance of privacy and the potential risks of sharing such information.

5. ***Monitor friend requests and followers:*** Help your child understand the importance of accepting friend requests or followers only from people they know and trust in real life. Encourage them to decline requests from unknown or suspicious accounts.

6. ***Online behaviour and etiquette:*** Teach your child about responsible online behaviour, emphasizing the importance of treating others with respect and kindness. Encourage them to think before they post or comment and avoid engaging in cyberbullying or spreading harmful content.

7. ***Regular communication:*** Maintain open lines of communication with your child about their social media activities. Encourage them to share any concerns or incidents they may encounter online. Be supportive and offer guidance whenever necessary.

8. ***Time management:*** Set boundaries on how much your child spends on social media. Encourage a healthy balance between online and offline activities. Discuss the potential negative impacts of excessive screen time and promote other hobbies and interests.

9. ***Regular monitoring:*** Regularly check your child's social media profiles and online activities. This will help you stay aware of the content they are sharing, their interactions, and any potential risks they may be exposed to.

10. ***Report and block:*** Teach your child to report and block individuals who engage in inappropriate or harmful online activities. Make sure they understand the reporting

mechanisms provided by social media platforms and how to use them effectively.

By following these tips and actively engaging with your child's social media presence, you can help create a safer and more positive online experience for them.

Section 2: Creating a Plan for Addressing Major Issues

Addressing cyberbullying and online harassment again in a list view

Cyberbullying and online harassment are significant concerns regarding children's online safety. Here are some important points to consider:

1. *Define cyberbullying:* Make sure your child understands what cyberbullying is. Explain that it involves using digital technologies, such as social media, messaging apps, or online platforms, to harass, intimidate, or harm others repeatedly.

2. *Open communication:* Encourage your child to talk openly about their online experiences and any incidents of cyberbullying or harassment they may encounter. Create a safe space where they feel comfortable sharing their concerns.

3. *Recognize the signs:* Educate your child about the signs of cyberbullying, such as sudden changes in mood, reluctance to use electronic devices, withdrawal from social activities,

or a decline in academic performance. Encourage them to be aware of their own emotions and reactions.

4. *Respond calmly and supportively:* If your child experiences cyberbullying, it is important to remain calm and supportive. Offer comfort and reassurance, and let them know they can rely on you for help. Avoid blaming or shaming them, as it is essential to create a non-judgmental environment.

5. *Document evidence:* Teach your child to save any evidence of cyberbullying or online harassment, such as screenshots, messages, or other relevant information. This evidence can be important if you must report the incident to the appropriate authorities or the platform.

6. *Block and report:* Instruct your child on how to block or unfriend the individuals involved in cyberbullying. Encourage them to report the incident to the social media platform or website where it occurred. Most platforms have reporting mechanisms to address such issues.

7. *Report to school or authorities:* If the cyberbullying involves someone from your child's school, inform the school administration or the appropriate authority. They can take action and provide support. If the harassment includes threats or appears criminal, consider reporting it to law enforcement.

8. *Online etiquette and bystander intervention:* Teach your child the importance of treating others with respect online and encourage them to stand up against cyberbullying when they witness it. Discuss the role of bystanders in preventing and stopping such behaviour.

9. *Emotional well-being:* Help your child develop resilience and coping strategies to deal with cyberbullying. Encourage them to engage in offline activities that boost their self-esteem and well-being, such as hobbies, sports, or spending time with friends and family.

10. *Seek professional help if needed:* If your child is deeply affected by cyberbullying or is experiencing significant distress, consider seeking professional help from a counsellor, therapist, or other mental health experts who specialize in supporting children.

Remember, prevention is key. Regularly discuss online safety, responsible digital behaviour, and the potential risks of cyberbullying with your child. By staying engaged and informed, you can help protect them from cyberbullying and online harassment.

CHAPTER 5: PROTECTING AGAINST ONLINE PREDATORS

Section 1: Identifying Signs of Human Trafficking

Recognizing the signs of online grooming and exploitation for kids online in list view because it's too important and often missed.

Recognizing the signs of online grooming and exploitation is crucial to protect children from potential harm. Here are some signs that may indicate online grooming and exploitation:

1. ***Excessive secrecy:*** If your child becomes excessively secretive about their online activities, including hiding screens or devices, avoiding discussions about their online interactions, or abruptly closing browser windows or apps when you approach, it could be a sign that they are trying to conceal something.

2. ***Excessive time spent online:*** Pay attention to any significant changes in your child's online behaviour, such as spending excessive amounts of time online, especially during the late hours of the night. This may indicate engagement with an online predator or be manipulated into inappropriate interactions.

3. ***Emotional withdrawal or changes:*** Watch for sudden changes in your child's behaviour, mood, or emotional well-being. They may become more withdrawn, anxious, irritable, or display signs of depression. Online grooming

and exploitation can significantly impact a child's emotional state.

4. *Secrecy about online friends:* If your child avoids discussing their online friends or becomes defensive or evasive when asked about them, it could be a warning sign. Groomers often try to isolate children by discouraging them from sharing details about their interactions.

5. *Inappropriate gifts or messages:* Be alert to any unsolicited gifts, packages, or letters your child receives from unknown sources. Also, if your child starts receiving explicit or inappropriate messages, images, or videos, it may indicate grooming or exploitation.

6. *Change in online behaviour:* If your child suddenly starts using language, slang, or sexual references that are inappropriate for their age, it could be a red flag. Groomers may influence their behaviour and introduce them to explicit content.

7. *Secretive online accounts or multiple profiles:* Notice if your child has secret social media accounts or multiple profiles on the same platform. Groomers may create fake identities to deceive and manipulate children.

8. *Unexplained financial transactions:* Keep an eye on any unexplained financial transactions or sudden requests for money from your child. Groomers may use manipulation tactics, such as convincing the child to share personal or financial information or engaging them in fraudulent schemes.

9. *Unwillingness to attend social activities or meet friends:* If your child becomes increasingly resistant to participating in social activities or meeting friends outside of their online

interactions, it may indicate that they are being groomed to prioritize their online relationships over real-life connections.

10. *Inappropriate content on devices:* Check your child's devices for inappropriate or explicit content, including images, videos, or messages. The presence of such content may indicate that they have been exposed to grooming or exploitation.

If you notice any of these signs, remaining calm and approaching your child with care and support is important. Establish open lines of communication and let them know they can trust you. Report any suspicious activity or concerns to law enforcement and seek professional help from counsellors or organizations specializing in child protection.

Strategies for minimizing the risks of contact with strangers online

Minimizing the risks of contact with strangers online is crucial for children's safety. Here are some strategies to help reduce those risks:

1. *Communication and education:* Have open and ongoing conversations with your child about online safety. Teach them about the potential risks of interacting with strangers online and the importance of being cautious.

2. *Set clear rules and boundaries:* Establish clear guidelines for your child's online activities, including rules about whom they can communicate with online. Emphasize that they should never share personal information or meet someone they've only met online without your knowledge and permission.

3. *Privacy settings and profiles:* Help your child set up and manage their privacy settings on social media platforms and other online services. Ensure their profiles are private and only visible to trusted friends and family members.

4. *Friend and follower requests:* Teach your child to be selective about accepting friend or follower requests. Encourage them to only connect with people they know in real life and to decline requests from strangers or unfamiliar individuals.

5. *Monitor online activities:* Regularly monitor your child's online activities, including their social media interactions, messages, and the platforms they use. Keep an eye on their friend lists and followers to identify any unfamiliar or suspicious accounts.

6. *Encourage reporting:* Teach your child to report inappropriate or suspicious behaviour to you or a trusted adult. Ensure they understand how to report concerns to the platform or website where the incident occurred.

7. *Teach critical thinking skills:* Help your child develop critical thinking skills to evaluate online information and people they encounter. Teach them to question motives, be skeptical of requests for personal information, and recognize potential red flags.

8. *Online pseudonyms:* Encourage your child to use online pseudonyms or usernames that do not reveal their real identity. This can help protect their personal information and make it more difficult for strangers to identify them.

9. *Online activities in common areas:* Encourage your child to engage in online activities in common areas of the house, such as the living room or kitchen. This allows for better

supervision and reduces the chances of secretive or risky online behaviour.

10. ***Trust your instincts:*** As a parent or guardian, trust your instincts if something feels off or suspicious about your child's online interactions. Investigate further, ask questions, and take appropriate action to ensure their safety.

Remember, the key is to maintain open lines of communication, establish trust with your child, and provide them with the knowledge and tools to make safe choices online. Regularly revisit and reinforce these strategies to ensure their effectiveness over time.

Promoting healthy relationships and digital boundaries for kids online

Promoting healthy relationships and digital boundaries for kids online is essential to help them develop a positive and safe online presence. Here are some strategies to encourage healthy digital relationships and set boundaries:

1. ***Start conversations about healthy relationships:*** Have open discussions with your child about what healthy relationships look like online and offline. Teach them about respect, empathy, and kindness in their interactions with others, emphasizing the importance of treating people online as they would in person.

2. ***Establish digital boundaries:*** Help your child set clear boundaries for their online interactions. Teach them to prioritize their privacy and well-being. Discuss what information is appropriate to share online and what should remain private.

3. ***Teach consent and respectful communication:*** Emphasize the importance of obtaining consent before sharing or

reposting someone else's content, photos, or personal information. Encourage your child to communicate respectfully and avoid engaging in any form of cyberbullying, harassment, or trolling.

4. *Encourage critical thinking and media literacy:* Teach your child to critically evaluate online content, including messages, posts, and news articles. Help them recognize and question false information, biased perspectives, and potentially harmful content.

5. *Set screen time limits:* Establish healthy screen time limits for your child and encourage them to engage in offline activities, such as hobbies, physical exercise, reading, or spending time with family and friends. Balancing online and offline activities is important for their overall well-being.

6. *Model healthy digital behaviour:* Be a positive role model by demonstrating healthy digital habits. Show your child how to use technology responsibly, engage in respectful online conversations, and maintain a healthy balance between online and offline activities.

7. *Monitor online activities:* Regularly check your child's online activities and conversations to ensure their safety. Use parental controls or monitoring software if necessary, but balance it with trust and open communication. Let your child know that you are there to support and guide them.

8. *Encourage reporting of inappropriate behaviour:* Teach your child to report any inappropriate behaviour or interactions they encounter online. Ensure they know how to report concerns to you, a trusted adult, or the appropriate platform or website.

9. *Foster offline relationships and activities:* Encourage your child to cultivate and nurture real-life relationships. Encourage participation in extracurricular activities, clubs, sports teams, or community events to build social connections beyond the digital realm.

10. *Stay updated on technology and platforms:* Stay informed about the latest social media platforms, apps, and online trends. This knowledge will enable you to guide your child effectively, understand potential risks, and provide relevant advice.

By implementing these strategies, you can help your child develop healthy digital habits, establish appropriate boundaries, and foster positive relationships in the online world.

CHAPTER 6: SCREEN TIME AND DIGITAL BALANCE

Section 1: The Negative Effects of Screen Time and Solutions

The impact of excessive screen time on children's well-being

Excessive screen time can have various implications for children's well-being. Here are some potential effects to consider:

1. *Physical health issues:* Excessive screen time often leads to a sedentary lifestyle, reducing physical activity levels. This can contribute to weight gain, obesity, and related health issues like cardiovascular problems, poor posture, and musculoskeletal disorders.

2. *Sleep disturbances:* Spending too much time on screens, especially close to bedtime, can disrupt sleep patterns. The blue light emitted by screens can interfere with the body's natural sleep-wake cycle, making it harder for children to fall asleep and obtain quality sleep.

3. *Mental and emotional well-being:* Excessive screen time has been associated with mental health issues such as anxiety, depression, and decreased self-esteem. It can lead to social isolation, as excessive screen use may replace face-to-face interactions and real-life social connections.

4. *Academic performance:* Spending excessive screen time can impact children's academic performance. It can reduce their ability to concentrate, focus, and retain information.

Excessive screen time may also lead to decreased time spent on homework, reading, or engaging in other intellectually stimulating activities.

5. *Language and cognitive development:* Excessive screen time can hinder language and cognitive development in young children. It may limit opportunities for interactive, hands-on play, conversation, and exploration crucial for healthy brain development.

6. *Behavioral issues:* Studies suggest excessive screen time is linked to behavioural problems such as attention deficits, impulsivity, and aggression in children. It can also contribute to a lack of self-regulation skills and an increased risk of developing addictive behaviours.

7. *Poor social skills:* Spending excessive time on screens can reduce opportunities for face-to-face social interactions and hinder the development of essential social skills. Children may struggle with empathy, communication, conflict resolution, and building meaningful relationships.

8. *Risky online behaviour:* Excessive screen time increases the likelihood of encountering inappropriate content or engaging in risky online activities. It may expose children to cyberbullying, online predators, and potential exploitation.

It's important to note that not all screen time is equal, and the content and context of screen use matter. Engaging in educational and age-appropriate content, supervised screen time, and balanced use can help mitigate some of the negative effects. Establishing clear screen time limits and encouraging a variety of offline activities can promote healthier well-being for children.

Setting boundaries and establishing healthy digital habits for kids online

Setting boundaries and establishing healthy digital habits for kids online is essential for their well-being and safety. Here are some strategies to help achieve this:

1. *Set clear screen time limits:* Establish specific rules around screen time, including the duration and times when screens are allowed. Consider using parental control tools or apps to manage and enforce these limits.

2. *Create tech-free zones and times:* Designate certain areas or times in your home as tech-free, such as during meals or in bedrooms before bedtime. This promotes unplugged activities and encourages face-to-face interactions.

3. *Lead by example:* Be a role model for healthy digital habits. Show your child that you prioritize offline activities, limit screen time, and engage in meaningful interactions without relying solely on technology.

4. *Encourage a variety of activities:* Encourage your child to participate in a range of activities beyond screens, such as sports, hobbies, arts and crafts, reading, and spending time outdoors. Help them discover and develop their interests offline.

5. *Foster offline social connections:* Promote and support your child's real-life social interactions. Encourage them to spend time with friends, join clubs or teams, and participate in community events. Balancing online and offline socializing is crucial for their social development.

6. *Create a device-free bedtime routine:* Establish a consistent and device-free bedtime routine to help your

child wind down before sleep. This can include activities like reading, storytelling, or relaxation techniques to promote better sleep quality.

7. *Teach responsible online behaviour:* Teach your child about responsible digital behaviour, including the importance of privacy, appropriate communication, and respectful interactions online. Help them understand the potential consequences of sharing personal information or engaging in cyberbullying.

8. *Establish media-free family activities:* Plan regular family activities or outings that do not involve screens. This could include board game nights, outdoor adventures, cooking together, or having quality family conversations.

9. *Monitor online activities:* Keep an eye on your child's online activities without invading their privacy. Monitor their social media accounts, friend lists, and online interactions to ensure their safety and guide them when needed.

10. *Have open conversations:* Maintain open lines of communication with your child about their online experiences. Encourage them to share concerns, incidents, or questions and provide guidance and support.

Remember that each child is unique, so adapt these strategies to their age, maturity level, and individual needs. Regularly revisit and reinforce these boundaries and habits to establish a healthy digital lifestyle for your child.

Eencourage offline activities and quality family time

Encouraging offline activities and quality family time is important for children's well-being and healthy development. Here are some strategies to promote these activities:

1. *Establish dedicated family time:* Set aside specific times for quality family time during the week. This could be a designated family game night, cooking together, going for walks or outings, or engaging in shared hobbies or interests.

2. *Create technology-free zones:* Designate certain areas or times in your home where technology is not allowed. This could be the dining table during meals or the living room during family activities. Encourage conversation and engagement without the distraction of screens.

3. *Plan outdoor activities:* Encourage outdoor activities that the whole family can participate in, such as hiking, biking, playing sports, or going to the park. Spending time in nature promotes physical activity, reduces screen time, and provides opportunities for exploration and bonding.

4. *Explore shared hobbies or interests:* Identify hobbies or activities the family can enjoy together. It could be cooking, gardening, art projects, DIY crafts, or even starting a family book club. Engaging in shared interests fosters connection and creates lasting memories.

5. *Set aside dedicated reading time:* Encourage reading as a family by designating regular reading time. Each family member can choose a book, and you can read silently together or take turns reading aloud. This promotes literacy, imagination, and relaxation.

6. ***Plan regular family outings:*** Schedule outings to museums, theatres, zoos, or local events that the whole family can attend. Experiencing new places and activities together creates shared experiences and strengthens family bonds.

7. ***Limit screen time during family activities:*** During family time, establish rules or agreements to limit the use of screens, including smartphones, tablets, and TVs. This ensures that everyone is fully engaged and present at the moment.

8. ***Encourage creative play and imagination:*** Provide materials and opportunities for creative play, such as building blocks, arts and crafts supplies, or dress-up costumes. Encourage imaginative play and storytelling, which helps develop cognitive skills and fosters creativity.

9. ***Involve children in household tasks:*** Include children in age-appropriate household tasks and chores. This not only helps lighten the workload but also teaches responsibility, teamwork, and life skills. Make these tasks enjoyable by turning them into a family activity.

10. ***Emphasize the importance of downtime:*** Teach your children the value of rest and relaxation. Encourage them to engage in activities that help them unwind, such as drawing, listening to music, or practicing mindfulness. Create a calm and peaceful environment at home to facilitate relaxation.

By prioritizing offline activities and quality family time, you can create a balanced and nurturing environment for your children, fostering their emotional well-being, communication skills, and family connections.

CHAPTER 7: EMPOWERING CHILDREN WITH CYBERSECURITY SKILLS

Section 1: Cybersecurity Skills for Kids

Tell children about safe internet browsing and avoiding malicious websites

When it comes to safe internet browsing and avoiding malicious websites, it's important to educate children about potential risks and provide them with strategies to protect themselves. Here are some key points to discuss with children:

1. *Explain the concept of malicious websites:* Start by explaining what malicious websites are. Let them know that these websites are designed to harm or exploit users by spreading malware, collecting personal information, or engaging in fraudulent activities.

2. *Use child-friendly language:* Tailor your explanations to your child's age and understanding. Use language that is age-appropriate and easy for them to grasp. You can use analogies or examples to help illustrate the concepts.

3. *Teach them to recognize trustworthy websites:* Help your child identify trustworthy websites. Teach them to look for well-known and reputable sources, such as educational institutions, government websites, or established organizations. Encourage them to rely on reliable search engines for information.

4. *Discuss the importance of web addresses:* Explain the significance of web addresses (URLs) in determining the legitimacy of a website. Teach them to verify the website's authenticity by looking for secure connections (https://) and familiar domain names (e.g., .org, .gov, .edu).

5. *Advise against clicking on suspicious links:* Teach your child to be cautious about clicking on unfamiliar links, especially those received through emails, social media messages, or unknown sources. Emphasize the importance of not opening attachments or downloading files from untrusted sources.

6. *Use web filters and parental control tools:* Install web filters and parental control tools to help block access to potentially harmful websites. These tools can help filter out inappropriate content and provide an additional layer of protection.

7. *Encourage reporting:* Let your child know they can approach you or a trusted adult if they encounter suspicious or inappropriate content online. Encourage them to report it immediately so that appropriate action can be taken.

8. *Teach them to avoid sharing personal information:* Emphasize the importance of never sharing personal information, such as full name, address, phone number, or passwords, on websites or with strangers online. Remind them that reputable websites and organizations will never ask for such information.

9. *Discuss online advertisements:* Teach your child to be skeptical of online advertisements and pop-up windows. Explain that they should not click on suspicious ads or offer

deals that seem too good to be true, as they may lead to malicious websites.

10. ***Encourage critical thinking:*** Teach your child to think critically when browsing the internet. Help them develop a healthy skepticism and question the credibility of information they come across. Encourage them to cross-reference information from multiple sources before accepting it as true.

By discussing these points with your child and reinforcing safe internet browsing habits, you can help them develop the necessary skills to navigate the online world safely and avoid potentially malicious websites.

Ppromote the use of strong and unique passwords.

Promoting strong and unique passwords is crucial for protecting online accounts and personal information. Here are some strategies to help children understand the importance of strong passwords and create unique ones:

1. ***Explain the purpose of strong passwords:*** Explain why strong passwords are necessary. Help children understand that strong passwords make it harder for others to guess or crack their accounts, protecting their personal information and online privacy.

2. ***Use the "password is like a lock" analogy:*** Compare passwords to locks on doors or safes. Just as a strong lock is harder to break, a strong password provides a higher level of security for their online accounts.

3. ***Teach the components of a strong password:*** Help children create passwords that are difficult to guess by using a combination of uppercase and lowercase letters,

numbers, and special characters. Encourage them to use a mix of these elements to increase complexity.

4. ***Emphasize password length:*** Teach children that longer passwords are generally more secure. Encourage them to create passwords that are at least eight characters long, but longer is even better.

5. ***Encourage unique passwords for each account:*** Explain the importance of using different passwords for different accounts. Using the same password for multiple accounts can increase the risk of all accounts being compromised if one password is breached.

6. ***Avoid obvious and easily guessable passwords:*** Teach children to avoid using obvious or easily guessable passwords, such as their names, birthdates, or common words. Help them understand that these passwords are vulnerable to being cracked by hackers.

7. ***Use password managers:*** Introduce password manager tools to your child. These tools can securely store and generate strong passwords for different accounts, making it easier to maintain unique passwords without remembering them all.

8. ***Help them create memorable passwords:*** Encourage children to create passwords that are memorable to them but difficult for others to guess. They can consider using a passphrase or a combination of words and numbers that have personal meaning but are not easily associated with their personal information.

9. ***Regularly update passwords:*** Teach children the importance of regularly updating their passwords, ideally

every few months or as recommended by the websites or services they use. This helps ensure ongoing security.

10. *Lead by example:* Practice what you preach using strong and unique passwords for your accounts. Children often learn by observing their parents or guardians, so set a good example regarding password security.

By promoting the use of strong and unique passwords, you can instill good security practices in your child from an early age, helping them protect their online accounts and personal information.

EExplain to children about phishing, scams, and malware

Explaining phishing, scams, and malware to children is important to help them understand potential online threats and how to protect themselves. Here's how you can explain these concepts to children:

1. *Define phishing:* Explain that phishing is when someone tries to trick or deceive people into revealing their personal information, such as passwords, usernames, or credit card details. Assure them that reputable organizations will never ask for this information through email, text messages, or online messages.

2. *Teach them about scams:* Explain that scams are fraudulent schemes designed to trick people into giving away their money or personal information. Inform them about common scams, such as lottery scams, inheritance scams, or online shopping scams, and teach them to be skeptical of any suspicious offers or requests for money.

3. *Discuss malware:* Describe malware as harmful software that can damage computers, steal personal information, or disrupt normal operations. Explain that malware can be hidden in email attachments, downloads, or infected

websites, and it's important to be cautious when clicking on unfamiliar links or downloading files.

4. *Emphasize the importance of not clicking on unknown links:* Teach children to be wary of clicking on links received through email, instant messages, or social media platforms if they are unsure of the sender's identity or the purpose of the link. Encourage them to ask for your assistance or guidance when encountering such situations.

5. *Teach them to recognize warning signs:* Help children recognize common warning signs of phishing or scams, such as poor grammar or spelling in emails, requests for personal information, urgent or threatening messages, or offers that seem too good to be true. Explain that they should be cautious and seek adult assistance if they receive such messages or requests.

6. *Stress the importance of not sharing personal information:* Remind children that they should never share personal information, such as full names, addresses, phone numbers, or passwords, with strangers online. Teach them that trustworthy websites and organizations will never ask for this information and that keeping personal details private is important.

7. *Encourage reporting:* Teach children to report suspicious emails, messages, or online activities to a trusted adult. Emphasize that it's better to be safe and ask for help rather than risk falling victim to phishing, scams, or malware.

8. *Use age-appropriate examples and language:* Tailor your explanations to your child's age and understanding. Use relatable examples and simple language to help them grasp the concepts and potential risks.

9. ***Regularly reinforce online safety practices:*** Remind
    children regularly about the importance of being cautious
    online and avoiding phishing, scams, and malware.
    Encourage open communication and assure them they can
    always approach you or a trusted adult for help or
    guidance.

By discussing phishing, scams, and malware with children, you can
help them develop a sense of online safety and empower them to
make informed decisions while navigating the digital world.

CHAPTER 8: THE ROLE OF PARENTAL CONTROLS AND MONITORING

Section 1: How to become the Chief Security Officer of your Home

Parental control features and monitoring tools

Parental control features and monitoring tools can be valuable resources for parents to ensure their children's safety and responsible use of technology. Here are some commonly available features and tools:

1. *Content filtering:* Parental control software or built-in device features allow you to block or filter inappropriate content, such as explicit websites or age-inappropriate apps. This helps create a safer online environment for children.

2. *Time limits and scheduling:* Parental control tools enable you to set time limits on device usage, specifying the amount of time your child can spend online. You can also schedule device access, restricting use during specific hours, such as bedtime or study time.

3. *App and website restrictions:* These features allow you to control which apps and websites your child can access. You can block or allow specific apps or websites based on their age appropriateness and your preferences.

4. *Safe search settings:* Many search engines offer safe filters blocking explicit content from search results. Enable safe browser search settings to ensure your child's online searches are filtered appropriately.

5. *Social media monitoring:* Some parental control tools offer features to monitor your child's social media activity, including monitoring their posts, messages, and friend requests. This allows you to monitor their online interactions and address any concerns.

6. *Location tracking:* Some parental control apps include GPS tracking capabilities, allowing you to track your child's whereabouts. This can help ensure their safety and know their location in real time.

7. *Usage reports and activity logs:* Monitoring tools provide usage reports and activity logs, giving insights into your child's online activities. You can review their browsing history, app usage, and overall screen time to identify any concerning patterns or potential risks.

8. *Remote device management:* You can remotely manage and control your child's devices with certain parental control tools. This includes features like locking or unlocking devices, remotely installing or removing apps, or adjusting settings from your device.

9. *Communication and alerts:* Parental control tools often allow for communication and alerts between parents and children. You can send messages, reminders, or notifications to your child's device and receive alerts if certain activities or keywords are detected.

10. *Open communication and trust-building:* While parental control features and monitoring tools can be helpful, it's

important to balance them with open communication and trust-building with your child. Discuss the purpose of these tools, explain the importance of responsible online behaviour, and involve them in setting boundaries and expectations.

Remember that parental control features and monitoring tools should be used in conjunction with ongoing conversations, education, and guidance about responsible internet use. They are tools to support your child's online safety, but fostering trust and open communication is equally important in ensuring their well-being in the digital world.

Iimplement age-appropriate restrictions and content filters

Implementing age-appropriate restrictions and content filters is essential for creating a safe and suitable online environment for children. Here are some guidelines for setting up these restrictions:

1. *Understand age appropriateness:* Familiarize yourself with age-specific guidelines and recommendations for online content. Different organizations and experts provide guidance on what is suitable for other age groups. Use these guidelines as a starting point for determining appropriate restrictions and filters.

2. *Utilize parental control software:* Install parental control software or use built-in parental control features available on devices and operating systems. These tools typically offer options for filtering content based on age and category, allowing you to customize settings according to your child's age and maturity level.

3. *Enable safe search settings:* Enable secure search settings on search engines to filter out explicit or inappropriate content from search results. Most popular search engines

offer this feature, which helps ensure that your child's online searches yield appropriate and safe results.

4. *Block explicit websites:* Use content filtering features to block access to explicit websites, adult content, violence, or other inappropriate materials. Parental control tools allow you to create blocklists or utilize pre-defined categories to restrict access to websites unsuitable for children.

5. *Set up app and game restrictions:* Enable app and game restrictions to prevent access to age-inappropriate applications or games. Many devices and operating systems have settings that allow you to restrict downloads or access based on age ratings or content categories.

6. *Regularly update filtering settings:* As your child grows older, review and update the filtering settings to align with their changing needs and developmental stages. What was appropriate for a younger child may not be sufficient for an older child. Stay involved and adapt the restrictions accordingly.

7. *Test and review the effectiveness:* Regularly test and review the effectiveness of your content filters and restrictions. Ensure that the filtering tools are accurately blocking inappropriate content and are not overly restrictive, preventing access to legitimate resources or educational content.

8. *Monitor and supervise:* While content filters are helpful, they are not foolproof. Maintain an active role in monitoring your child's online activities, especially for younger children. Regularly discuss their internet use, ask about their online experiences, and address any concerns or questions they may have.

9. *Teach responsible internet use:* Teach your child about responsible internet use, appropriate online behaviour, and the potential risks they may encounter. Help them understand why content filters and restrictions are in place and the importance of following these guidelines.

10. *Adjust gradually:* Gradually adjust the restrictions and content filters as your child demonstrates responsible online behaviour and maturity. Allow them to earn more independence and gradually expand their online access while continuing to provide guidance and support.

Remember, implementing age-appropriate restrictions and content filters should accompany open communication and ongoing conversations about online safety. It is important to empower children with the knowledge and skills to navigate the online world responsibly as they grow.

Balancing privacy and safety concerns online

Balancing privacy and safety concerns online is crucial in ensuring a positive online experience for children. Here are some strategies to help achieve this balance:

1. *Educate children about privacy:* Teach children about the importance of personal privacy and the potential risks of sharing sensitive information online. Help them understand what information is considered private, such as full name, address, phone number, school name, and passwords. Encourage them to be cautious when sharing personal information and to only do so with trusted individuals or on secure platforms.

2. *Set privacy settings:* Review and adjust privacy settings on social media platforms, online accounts, and devices to maximize privacy. Enable features that limit who can view

and interact with your child's online content and information. Teach children how to manage their privacy settings as they get older.

3. *Teach critical thinking:* Help children develop critical thinking skills to evaluate online requests for personal information or suspicious messages. Teach them to question and verify the legitimacy of requests before sharing any personal details. Encourage them to ask for your guidance or assistance when in doubt.

4. *Maintain open communication:* Create an environment of trust and open communication where children feel comfortable discussing their online activities, concerns, and experiences. Let them know they can approach you if they encounter any uncomfortable situations or if their privacy feels compromised.

5. *Monitor online activities:* Regularly monitor your child's online activities, especially for younger children. Be aware of the websites they visit, the apps they use, and the people they interact with. Use parental control tools and monitoring features to ensure their safety while respecting their privacy appropriately.

6. *Teach responsible social media use:* Educate children about responsible social media use, including being mindful of the content they post and share. Discuss the potential long-term consequences of sharing inappropriate or compromising information online, such as the impact on their reputation or future opportunities.

7. *Encourage safe and private communication:* Teach children to communicate with friends and acquaintances using secure and private platforms, such as direct

messaging or private group chats, rather than publicly sharing personal information. Emphasize the importance of being selective about the individuals they connect with online.

8. ***Model good online behaviour:*** Be a positive role model by practicing good online behaviour yourself. Demonstrate responsible use of social media, respect for privacy, and thoughtful sharing of personal information. Children often learn by observing their parents or guardians, so leading by example is essential.

9. ***Foster digital literacy:*** Help children develop digital literacy skills to understand the risks and challenges of the online world. Teach them about online threats, scams, and strategies for protecting their privacy. Encourage them to critically evaluate online content, identify misinformation, and navigate privacy settings effectively.

10. ***Stay informed and up-to-date:*** Stay informed about the latest online privacy issues, trends, and best practices. Be proactive in learning about new technologies and platforms your child may use to understand their privacy implications better.

By balancing privacy and safety concerns, you can empower children to navigate the online world responsibly while protecting their personal information and maintaining a positive digital footprint. Regularly reassess and adjust strategies as your child grows and their online activities evolve.

CHAPTER 9: RESPONDING TO CYBERSECURITY INCIDENTS

Section 1: Key Steps to Follow When Problems Arise

Steps to take if your child becomes a victim of cyberbullying or harassment

If your child becomes a victim of cyberbullying or online harassment, it's crucial to take immediate action to address the situation and provide support. Here are the steps you can take:

1. *Stay calm and supportive:* Reassure your child that they are not alone and that you are there to help and support them. Encourage open communication and create a safe space to express their feelings and concerns.

2. *Document evidence:* Advise your child to save and document any evidence of cyberbullying or harassment, such as screenshots, messages, or other relevant information. This evidence can be useful when reporting the incident to the appropriate authorities or platforms.

3. *Encourage your child not to respond:* Advise your child not to engage with the cyberbully or harasser. Responding to negative or hurtful messages can escalate the situation and give the perpetrator the attention they seek. Instead, focus on blocking or ignoring the individual.

4. *Report the incident:* Help your child report the incident to the relevant authorities or platforms where cyberbullying or harassment occurs. This may include reporting to the

school administration, social media platforms, online gaming communities, or local law enforcement, depending on the severity and nature of the incident.

5. ***Preserve evidence with platforms:*** If cyberbullying or harassment occurs on social media platforms or online communities, report the incident to the platform's administrators. Provide them with your collected evidence and ask for their assistance addressing the situation.

6. ***Inform the school:*** If the cyberbullying involves classmates or peers, notify the school administration or counsellor about the situation. Share the evidence you have collected and work together to develop a plan to address the issue, ensuring the school takes appropriate action.

7. ***Support your child's emotional well-being:*** Cyberbullying can significantly impact children emotionally and psychologically. Provide emotional support, listen to their concerns, and validate their feelings. Encourage them to engage in activities they enjoy and seek professional help if needed, such as counselling or therapy.

8. ***Encourage safe online practices:*** Remind your child about the importance of safe online practices, such as not sharing personal information, being cautious about accepting friend requests or messages from unknown individuals, and reporting suspicious or harmful behaviour.

9. ***Communicate with other parents:*** If cyberbullying involves other children, consider contacting their parents to discuss the issue. Approaching the situation calmly and constructively can help foster understanding and collaboration in addressing the problem.

10. **Document ongoing incidents:** Keep a record of any further incidents or interactions related to cyberbullying. This documentation will be useful if other actions, such as obtaining a restraining order or involving legal authorities, need to be taken.

Remember, addressing cyberbullying requires a multi-faceted approach involving the cooperation of parents, schools, and online platforms. Your child's well-being and safety should always be the top priority, so continue to provide support and take appropriate actions to protect them from further harm.

Section 2: Addressing Other Important Security Concerns

Dealing with identity theft and online fraud

Dealing with identity theft and online fraud can be a stressful experience. Here are steps to take if you suspect your child's identity has been compromised or if they become a victim of online fraud:

1. **Act quickly:** Time is of the essence when dealing with identity theft or online fraud. If you suspect any suspicious activity, take immediate action to minimize the potential damage.

2. **Notify the authorities:** Report the incident to your local law enforcement agency and provide them with all the relevant details. They can guide you on the appropriate steps to take and may launch an investigation if necessary.

3. ***Contact financial institutions:*** If financial accounts or credit cards are involved, contact your bank, credit card companies, and any other financial institutions your child has accounts with. Inform them about the situation and request a freeze on the accounts to prevent any unauthorized transactions.

4. ***Change passwords and secure accounts:*** Advise your child to change passwords for all their online accounts, including email, social media, and banking accounts. Encourage them to use strong, unique passwords and enable two-factor authentication whenever possible.

5. ***Monitor accounts and credit reports:*** Regularly monitor your child's financial accounts and credit reports for any suspicious activity. You can request a free credit report from the major credit bureaus to check for any unauthorized charges or credit inquiries in your child's name.

6. ***Contact credit bureaus:*** Contact the credit bureaus (Equifax, Experian, and TransUnion) to report the identity theft and place a fraud alert or credit freeze on your child's credit file. This makes it more difficult for identity thieves to open new accounts in their name.

7. ***Report to relevant organizations:*** If the incident involves a specific website, social media platform, or online service, report the fraud or identity theft to them. They may be able to investigate the issue and take appropriate actions to address it.

8. ***Keep records and document everything:*** Maintain a detailed record of all communications, transactions, and interactions related to identity theft or online fraud. This

documentation can be helpful for law enforcement, financial institutions, or credit bureaus during the investigation process.

9. *Educate your child about online safety:* Use the incident as an opportunity to educate your child about online safety practices. Teach them about the importance of protecting their personal information, being cautious about sharing sensitive data online, and recognizing signs of phishing or fraudulent activities.

10. *Consider professional assistance:* If the identity theft or online fraud is extensive or complex, you may want to seek professional assistance from identity theft protection services or legal professionals who specialize in these matters. They can guide you through the process and provide expert advice.

Remember, prevention is key when it comes to identity theft and online fraud. Encourage your child to practice safe online habits, such as being cautious with sharing personal information, using secure connections, and regularly monitoring their online accounts.

Rreporting incidents and seeking help from authorities and support organizations

Reporting incidents and seeking help from authorities and support organizations is crucial in addressing online safety concerns for children. Here are steps to take when reporting incidents and seeking assistance:

1. *Document evidence:* Collect and document any evidence related to the incident, such as screenshots, messages, emails, or other relevant information. This evidence will be important when reporting the incident and seeking help.

2. ***Report to local authorities:*** If the incident involves illegal activities, such as threats, harassment, or explicit content, report it to your local law enforcement agency. Provide them with all the evidence you have collected and explain the situation. They will guide you on the appropriate steps to take and may launch an investigation if necessary.

3. ***Contact your child's school:*** If the incident involves peers or classmates, inform your child's school administration, counsellor, or a trusted teacher about the situation. Share the evidence and details of the incident with them so that they can take appropriate action within the school community.

4. ***Report to online platforms:*** If the incident occurs on social media platforms, gaming communities, or other online platforms, report it to the platform's administrators. Most platforms have reporting mechanisms in place for various types of abuse or inappropriate behaviour. Follow their guidelines and provide the necessary information to report the incident.

5. ***Seek support from support organizations:*** Reach out to support organizations that specialize in online safety, cyberbullying, or child protection. These organizations can provide you and your child with guidance, resources, and support. They can help you understand the available options and connect you with appropriate services.

6. ***Use helpline services:*** Many countries have helpline services dedicated to assisting children and families in cases of online abuse or safety concerns. Look for helpline numbers or online chat services that you can contact for immediate assistance and guidance.

7. ***Involve child protection agencies:*** If the incident involves serious threats, exploitation, or child endangerment, consider involving child protection agencies in your jurisdiction. They have expertise in handling such cases and can take appropriate measures to ensure your child's safety.

8. ***Support groups and counselling:*** Seek out support groups or counselling services that specialize in dealing with the emotional and psychological impact of online safety incidents. These services can provide a safe space for your child to express their feelings, share their experiences, and receive guidance and support.

9. ***Follow up and stay vigilant:*** Keep a record of all the reports made and maintain open communication with the authorities, school, and support organizations. Stay vigilant in monitoring your child's online activities and promptly address future incidents.

Remember, reporting incidents and seeking help is essential for the well-being and safety of your child. Encourage them to speak up about any concerning experiences and assure them they are not alone in dealing with these issues.

CHAPTER 10: CULTIVATING RESILIENCE AND DIGITAL WELL-BEING

Section 1: Tips to Keep Online Fun and Safe

How to nurture emotional resilience in the face of online challenges

Fostering emotional resilience in the face of online challenges is important for children to confidently navigate the digital world and cope with any difficulties they may encounter. Here are some strategies to foster emotional resilience:

1. ***Open communication:*** Create a supportive and open environment where your child feels comfortable discussing their online experiences, challenges, and concerns. Encourage them to express their emotions and thoughts openly without judgment. Listen actively and validate their feelings.

2. ***Develop self-awareness:*** Help your child develop self-awareness by encouraging them to identify and understand their emotions and reactions to online challenges. Teach them to recognize how certain situations or interactions make them feel and why. This self-awareness can help them better manage their emotions.

3. ***Build self-esteem and self-worth:*** Foster a positive sense of self-esteem and self-worth in your child. Emphasize their strengths and achievements, both online and offline. Encourage them to focus on their abilities, talents, and

positive qualities rather than solely relying on external validation from the online world.

4. ***Encourage problem-solving skills:*** Teach your child problem-solving skills to tackle online challenges effectively. Help them identify different approaches, weigh the pros and cons, and make informed decisions. Encourage them to seek creative solutions and explore alternative perspectives.

5. ***Teach coping strategies:*** Equip your child with effective coping strategies to manage stress and adversity online. Encourage healthy outlets for stress, such as physical activities, hobbies, or spending time with supportive friends and family. Teach relaxation techniques, such as deep breathing or mindfulness, to manage feelings of anxiety or frustration.

6. ***Foster empathy and perspective-taking:*** Encourage your child to develop empathy by considering others' perspectives and feelings. Help them understand that everyone has different experiences and challenges online. This empathy can foster resilience and promote kindness and understanding in their interactions.

7. ***Set realistic expectations:*** Discuss with your child the importance of setting realistic expectations online. Help them understand that not everything they see or encounter accurately represents reality. Encourage them to focus on personal growth and learning rather than seeking validation or comparing themselves to others.

8. ***Develop critical thinking skills:*** Teach your child critical thinking skills to assess online content, including identifying misinformation, evaluating sources, and

questioning the credibility of information. This will help them navigate online challenges with a discerning and analytical mindset.

9. *Encourage digital breaks*: Promote regular digital breaks to give your child time to disconnect from online challenges and focus on other activities. Encourage them to engage in offline hobbies, spend time with friends and family, and enjoy nature. These breaks can provide a refreshing perspective and reduce the impact of online challenges.

10. *Model resilience:* Be a positive role model by demonstrating resilience in your own life. Show your child how you face challenges, overcome obstacles, and learn from setbacks. Share your own experiences of dealing with online challenges and how you managed to navigate them effectively.

Remember, building emotional resilience takes time and practice. Support your child consistently, provide guidance when needed, and celebrate their resilience and growth. By nurturing emotional resilience, you empower your child to face online challenges with confidence, adaptability, and a positive mindset.

Promoting positive digital citizenship and ethical behaviour online

Promoting positive digital citizenship and ethical behaviour online is crucial for children to become responsible and respectful digital world users. Here are some strategies to encourage positive digital citizenship:

1. *Model positive behaviour*: As a parent or guardian, be a positive role model for your child by demonstrating responsible and ethical behaviour online. Show them how

to engage respectfully with others, protect their privacy, and use technology responsibly.

2. *Teach digital etiquette:* Educate your child about the importance of digital etiquette or "netiquette." Teach them to use polite and respectful language, avoid engaging in online conflicts, and think before they post or comment. Encourage them to treat others online as they would in person.

3. *Foster empathy and kindness:* Emphasize the importance of compassion and kindness in online interactions. Encourage your child to consider the feelings and perspectives of others before posting or commenting. Remind them that their words and actions online can have a real impact on others.

4. *Discuss responsible use of social media:* Guide your child on responsible use of social media platforms. Teach them about privacy settings, the importance of not sharing personal information with strangers, and the potential consequences of posting inappropriate or harmful content. Encourage them to think critically about what they share and consider the potential impact on themselves and others.

5. *Promote critical thinking and media literacy:* Teach your child to critically evaluate online content, including news articles, videos, and social media posts. Help them develop media literacy skills to identify misinformation, verify sources, and differentiate between reliable and unreliable information. Encourage them to question and seek evidence before accepting information as true.

6. *Respect intellectual property:* Teach your child about copyright and intellectual property rights. Help them

understand the importance of crediting original creators, avoiding plagiarism, and seeking permission when using others' work or content. Encourage them to create and share their original content responsibly.

7. ***Encourage responsible digital footprint:*** Help your child understand the concept of a digital footprint and how their online actions leave a permanent trace. Teach them to be mindful of what they post and share, as it can impact their reputation and future opportunities. Encourage them to think long-term and consider the potential consequences of their online actions.

8. ***Discuss cyberbullying and online harassment:*** Have open and honest conversations with your child about cyberbullying and online harassment. Teach them to recognize the signs, how to report and block abusive behaviour, and the importance of standing up against cyberbullying. Encourage them to be allies to those targeted and seek help if they witness or experience such behaviour.

9. ***Set expectations and monitor online activities:*** Establish clear expectations and guidelines for your child's online activities. Set limits on screen time, establish rules around online behaviour, and regularly monitor their online interactions. This helps ensure their safety and provides an opportunity for ongoing discussions about responsible digital citizenship.

10. ***Stay involved and engaged:*** Stay involved in your child's online activities. Show interest in their digital experiences, ask questions about what they are doing online, and discuss any concerns or issues that may arise. You can provide

guidance and support and help shape their positive digital citizenship by staying engaged.

By promoting positive digital citizenship and ethical behaviour online, you can help your child navigate the digital world responsibly, contribute positively to online communities, and become good digital citizens who respect themselves and others.

Supporting mental health and promoting a healthy relationship with technology for kids

Supporting mental health and promoting a healthy relationship with technology is essential for children's overall well-being. Here are strategies to achieve this:

1. *Foster open communication:* Create a safe and non-judgmental environment where your child feels comfortable discussing their feelings and concerns about technology. Encourage honest conversations about the positive and negative aspects of technology and their online experiences.

2. *Set boundaries and limits:* Establish clear boundaries and limits around screen time and technology use. Work together with your child to define healthy and balanced habits. Encourage breaks from screens and engage in offline activities that promote physical activity, creativity, and social interactions.

3. *Encourage digital balance:* Help your child understand the importance of balance in their technology use. Encourage them to engage in a variety of activities both online and offline, such as hobbies, sports, reading, and spending time with family and friends. Emphasize the importance of moderation and avoiding excessive screen time.

4. *Promote self-care:* Teach your child the importance of self-care and maintaining a healthy online and offline lifestyle. Encourage them to prioritize activities that promote their physical, mental, and emotional well-being, such as getting enough sleep, eating nutritious meals, exercising, and practicing mindfulness or relaxation techniques.

5. *Educate about online content:* Teach your child to critically evaluate online content and be aware of its potential impact on their mental health. Discuss the importance of avoiding or minimizing exposure to harmful content, including excessive violence, explicit material, or toxic online communities. Encourage them to seek out positive, educational, and inspiring content.

6. *Encourage digital literacy:* Promote digital literacy skills in your child. Teach them to navigate the digital landscape responsibly, including understanding online privacy, recognizing and addressing cyberbullying or harassment, and being aware of online scams or malicious activities. Help them develop the skills to protect themselves and make informed decisions online.

7. *Model healthy technology use:* Be a positive role model for your child by demonstrating healthy technology use yourself. Show them how you use technology mindfully, such as setting boundaries, prioritizing offline activities, and maintaining healthy relationships. Children often mirror their parents' behaviours, so leading by example is powerful.

8. *Support offline social connections:* Encourage your child to build and maintain strong offline relationships. Foster opportunities for them to interact with friends, family, and their community through activities such as outings,

hobbies, or volunteering. Offline connections provide valuable social support and help balance their digital interactions.

9. ***Teach stress management techniques:*** Help your child develop effective stress management techniques to cope with the pressures of technology and online experiences. Teach them relaxation exercises, deep breathing, or mindfulness techniques that can help reduce stress and promote mental well-being.

10. ***Seek professional help if needed:*** If you notice persistent signs of distress, anxiety, or other mental health concerns in your child related to technology use, consider seeking professional help. A mental health professional can provide appropriate guidance and support tailored to your child's specific needs.

Remember, every child is unique, and finding the right balance with technology may require ongoing adjustment and open communication. By prioritizing mental health and promoting a healthy relationship with technology, you can help your child develop resilience, navigate the digital world responsibly, and maintain overall well-being.

SUPPORT, RESOURCES & ASSISTANCE

Cyberbullying

Several organizations provide support, resources, and assistance to individuals dealing with cyberbullying. These organizations aim to educate, raise awareness, and offer tools to prevent and address online harassment. Here are some notable organizations that help with cyberbullying:

1. **Cyberbullying Research Center:** This organization focuses on research, education, and outreach related to cyberbullying and online harassment. They provide educators, parents, and young people with resources to prevent and respond to cyberbullying.

2. **Stomp Out Bullying:** Stomp Out Bullying is a leading national anti-bullying and cyberbullying organization. They provide support, information, and resources for students, parents, and educators to address various forms of bullying.

3. **The Trevor Project:** While primarily focused on providing crisis intervention and suicide prevention services for LGBTQ+ youth, The Trevor Project also addresses cyberbullying and offers resources for dealing with online harassment.

4. **StopBullying.gov:** This U.S. government website provides information and resources related to bullying prevention, including cyberbullying. It guides parents, educators, and kids on recognizing, preventing, and responding to bullying.

5. **iKeepSafe:** The Internet Keep Safe Coalition educates parents, educators, and youth about online safety and

responsible digital citizenship. They offer resources on cyberbullying prevention and online etiquette.

6. **Ditch the Label:** Ditch the Label is an international anti-bullying charity that supports and advises young people facing various forms of bullying, including cyberbullying. They have a helpline and online resources.

7. **PACER's National Bullying Prevention Center:** PACER's center provides resources and support for bullying prevention, including cyberbullying. They offer toolkits, educational materials, and activities for schools and communities.

8. **Childnet International:** Childnet International is a UK-based organization that works to make the Internet a safe place for children and young people. They provide resources for children, parents, and educators to address online safety and cyberbullying.

9. **Bullying Canada:** This organization supports individuals affected by bullying, including cyberbullying, in Canada. They offer helplines, resources, and information for both youth and parents.

10. **Headspace:** While primarily focused on mental health support for young people, Headspace also provides information and advice on dealing with cyberbullying and online harassment.

Remember that the availability of organizations may vary based on your region or country. If you or someone you know is experiencing cyberbullying, reaching out to these organizations can provide valuable guidance and support.

Cyber Human Trafficking

Dealing with issues related to cyber human trafficking requires a comprehensive approach involving law enforcement, government agencies, and various non-governmental organizations. While there isn't a single organization exclusively focused on "cyber human trafficking," several organizations work to combat human trafficking in all its forms, including online exploitation. Here are some notable organizations that are involved in addressing human trafficking, including its digital aspects:

1. **Polaris:** Polaris is a leading organization combating human trafficking in the United States. They operate the National Human Trafficking Hotline, which assists victims and gathers data to understand trafficking trends, including those involving online exploitation.

2. **ECPAT International:** ECPAT is a global network of organizations dedicated to ending the sexual exploitation of children. They focus on raising awareness, advocating for policy changes, and supporting victims, including those targeted through online platforms.

3. **Thorn:** Thorn is a nonprofit organization that uses technology to address various forms of online child exploitation, including human trafficking. They collaborate with tech companies, law enforcement, and other organizations to develop tools and solutions to combat online abuse.

4. **Not For Sale:** Not For Sale works to end modern slavery and human trafficking globally. They focus on prevention, rescue, and survivor support, which includes addressing online exploitation.

5. **ECPAT-USA:** ECPAT-USA is part of the global ECPAT network and focuses on ending the sexual exploitation of children in the United States. They work to raise awareness, advocate for policy changes, and provide training and resources to various stakeholders.

6. **A21:** A21 is an international organization that aims to abolish modern slavery, including human trafficking. They support survivors, conduct awareness campaigns, and

collaborate with law enforcement agencies to combat trafficking.

7. **United Nations Office on Drugs and Crime (UNODC):** UNODC is crucial in addressing human trafficking globally. They provide resources, training, and support to member states to prevent trafficking and prosecute perpetrators.

8. **Coalition Against Trafficking in Women (CATW):** CATW is an international organization focused on combating the trafficking of women and girls for sexual exploitation. They work to raise awareness, advocate for policy changes, and provide support for survivors.

9. **Blue Campaign:** Run by the U.S. Department of Homeland Security, it focuses on raising public awareness and training law enforcement personnel to combat human trafficking, including its online components.

10. **National Center for Missing and Exploited Children (NCMEC):** NCMEC operates the CyberTipline, which allows individuals to report online child exploitation, including trafficking. They work with law enforcement to investigate and respond to reports.

Remember that addressing cyber human trafficking requires collaborative efforts among stakeholders, including law enforcement, government agencies, NGOs, and the private sector. If you encounter any suspicious online activity related to human trafficking, consider reporting it to the appropriate authorities or organizations in your region.

Cyber-inappropriate photos online.

Dealing with inappropriate photos online, often referred to as "revenge porn" or "non-consensual sharing of intimate images," is a serious issue that can have severe emotional and legal consequences. Several organizations work to provide support, resources, and assistance to individuals who are affected by this type of online harassment. Here are some organizations that help with dealing with inappropriate photos online:

1. **Cyber Civil Rights Initiative (CCRI):** CCRI is a nonprofit organization dedicated to combating online abuse, including sharing non-consensual intimate images. They provide resources, legal support, and advocacy for victims.

2. **Without My Consent:** Without My Consent focuses on combatting online invasions of privacy, including revenge porn. They offer information about legal rights, steps to take, and resources for victims.

3. **End Revenge Porn:** End Revenge Porn is a platform that offers information about laws and legal resources related to revenge porn in various countries. They aim to educate victims about their legal rights and options.

4. **Badass Army:** Badass Army is an organization that provides support for survivors of non-consensual image sharing and advocates for policy changes to address this issue.

5. **VictimConnect Resource Center:** VictimConnect offers support, resources, and information for victims of all types of crimes, including those affected by online harassment and intimate image sharing.

6. **Legal Aid Organizations:** Many legal aid organizations provide assistance to individuals dealing with online harassment and revenge porn. Search for legal aid organizations in your region that can provide advice and legal support.

7. **Local Law Enforcement:** If you believe a crime has been committed, including the non-consensual sharing of intimate images, consider reporting the incident to your local law enforcement agency.

8. **Online Safety Hotlines:** Many countries have online safety hotlines or helplines where you can report and seek guidance on online harassment issues. Look for the appropriate hotline in your country.

9. **Social Media Platforms:** If inappropriate photos are being shared on social media platforms, report the content to the platform administrators. They often have mechanisms for reporting and removing such content.

10. **Counseling and Mental Health Services:** Dealing with the emotional impact of inappropriate photos online can be challenging. Consider seeking counselling or mental health support to cope with the stress and emotional distress.

Remember that your safety and well-being are paramount. If you or someone you know is affected by inappropriate photos online, seeking help from the appropriate organizations and authorities can provide valuable assistance and guidance.

AFTERWORD

In closing, we reflect on the paramount importance of safeguarding our children's digital lives in the face of the modern age's most pressing challenges. Throughout this journey, we've explored the intricacies of cybersecurity, delved into the nuances of responsible digital citizenship, and equipped parents with invaluable tools to guide their children through the ever-evolving digital landscape.

The realities of our digital world can be both awe-inspiring and concerning. As technology continues shaping how we live and interact, we cannot ignore the darker corners it casts light upon. We've confronted issues such as revenge porn, cyberbullying, and human trafficking head-on, understanding that these topics demand our utmost attention and action.

Revenge porn, an unconscionable violation of privacy, underscores the urgency of teaching our children about consent, respect, and the potential consequences of sharing intimate content. Cyberbullying, often shrouded in anonymity, reveals the dark side of the internet's connectivity, emphasizing the need to foster empathy, resilience, and open communication within our families.

And then there's the chilling spectre of human trafficking, a horrifying reality that can exploit the innocence of our children. We've seen that predators can exploit vulnerabilities in the digital space to deceive and manipulate. We must arm our children with knowledge, critical thinking skills, and a vigilant awareness of their online interactions to combat this.

In addressing these challenges, this book reinforces that our role as parents is to protect and educate. By nurturing a strong bond built on trust, we can encourage our children to come to us with their concerns, to seek guidance when faced with the unfamiliar, and to stand up against online threats.

As our children grow and adapt to the digital world, so must our parenting approach. Just as we teach them to cross the street safely, we must teach them to navigate the intricate pathways of the internet. Our dedication to fostering a culture of digital responsibility will determine the legacy we leave for future generations.

In the end, we hope this book serves as a steadfast companion, a reference, and a source of inspiration for parents navigating the uncharted waters of cybersecurity with their children. By instilling in our young ones the values of empathy, discernment, and cautious exploration, we can collectively create a safer, more secure digital realm for them to thrive in. Remember, in the vast expanse of the digital universe, we are their steadfast guides, protectors, and unwavering advocates.

ABOUT THE AUTHOR

Gregory Dharma LePard has been active in Information Technology and Cybersecurity for over 20 years. He is an innovative and driven professional with a culmination of experience in Cybersecurity, Sales Engineering, Account Management and Ethical Hacking. With his passion for cybersecurity and the ever-evolving cybersecurity landscape, Gregory is always on the hunt for knowledge, and it shows he is continually getting certifications related to the cybersecurity field, giving him a wide breadth of knowledge, and he likes to share it!

Gregory is the co-founder and Chief Evangelist of Cybersnap - a cybersecurity consulting firm providing services from Cybersecurity Training, vCISO, and Cloud to Technical and Security Overviews and Ethical Hacking.

The philosophy of Cybersnap is that we want to bring the human element back to cybersecurity; it's the first line of defence.

Gregory lives in Canada with his spouse and fur baby.

ACKNOWLEDGEMENTS

"I must start by thanking Imogen Fannon. From reading early drafts to editing, suggesting cover and title options and designing the layout, she was as important to this book getting completed as I was.

I would also like to thank my family for their unwavering support and cheerleading, enabling me to take the leap and follow my dreams.

Thank you so much."

www.ingramcontent.com/pod-product-compliance
Lightning Source LLC
Chambersburg PA
CBHW062323290526
45794CB00005B/1881